Nurture Your Creative Spirit

Wisdom and Insight Learned Through the Art of Quilting

To all the ladies at Needlechasers Quilt Guild ~ May you be always inspired to create from your heart and soul. With love, Vikki

Vikki Pignatelli

Publisher: Vikki Pignatelli

Senior Technical Editor: Augustine Ellis

Book Cover and Graphic Design: Merry Yee Clark

Copy Editors: Marianne Beck and Lauretta Ellis

Photography: Dennis and Vikki Pignatelli

Author Photo: Dennis Pignatelli

First U.S. Edition published in 2012
Printed in the USA by
beckmanXMO, Columbus, OH

ISBN: 978-0-615-61794-7

© 2012 Vikki Pignatelli
All rights reserved. No part of this publication may be reproduced, photocopied, transmitted or replicated in any form or by any means including electronic, mechanical, recording or otherwise, in any information storage or retrieval system without the notification and written consent of the author and publisher, Vikki Pignatelli.

Cover Image: ***Promise of Spring*** (Detail)

Please note the material written in this book is solely the opinions and beliefs of the author. The advice offered is intended to provide helpful and thoughtful knowledge to the reader based on the experiences of the author. It is written with the understanding the writer is not engaged in providing professional services.

Summer's Bounty (Detail)

Acknowledgements

To my sister and senior editor, Augustine Ellis. I am forever grateful for your guidance, patience and wisdom, not only while working on this book, but throughout my life. You are always there and supportive when I need you and simple words cannot express how deeply appreciative I am for all you do.

Many thanks to Marianne Beck and Lauretta Ellis for their invaluable editing and proofreading expertise and suggestions. Through your efforts, *Nurture Your Creative Spirit* is a far better book.

To Merry Yee Clark, my graphic designer, your wonderful artistry and expertise has transformed a vision and a manuscript into a beautiful book. Thank you so much!

My deepest gratitude to my dear husband, Denny. I appreciate your patience, support, understanding and love. You enable me, allowing me to follow my heart and my mission. I thank God every day we are on life's journey together.

Dedication

Dedicated to the Sacred Spirit, inherent in all, who blesses us with creativity and endless opportunities to inspire the minds and hearts of others with a magnitude far beyond our dreams or human understanding.

Fire Within (Detail)

Table of Contents

Introduction — 8

The Improbable Quilter — 10

Traits That Nurture Creativity — 16

    Determination — 18
        Breaking Point
        Lightning Strikes Twice

    Persistence — 23
        Fire and Ice
        Aftermath

    Humor — 27
        Feelin' Groovy
        Blacklick Pond: Reflections At Twilight

    Flexibility — 31
        Against All Odds
        Red Sky at Night
        Tears On Blacklick Pond
        Silhouette

    Patience — 40
        Portrait of My Soul

    Courage — 50
        After the Storm
        Child's Play

    Curiosity — 53

    Have Faith In Yourself — 55
        Creation of the Sun and Stars

    The Story Behind Creation of the Sun and Stars — 60

    Passion — 65
        The Fire Within: Our Spirit of Creativity

    Ability to Share Your Work and Yourself — 71
        Resting Place

    Motivation — 76
        Pond Reflections at Dawn

Quilts are listed in italics

Creativity   84
    Rhapsody in Pink
    Rocky Mountain Wildflowers

Why Do We Create Art?   92
    Running in Circles
    November Moon

Emotions, Healing and Creativity   98
    Passages of the Spirit
    Hanging on for Dear Life
    Engulfed

Inspirations   109
    Life Beyond
    Summer's Bounty

Design Walls   118
    At Sea

A Tree of Many Colors   122
    The Promise of Spring
    Valley of Fire

The Spider's Web   129
    The Spider's Web

The Sequence of Creativity   132
    Log Cabin Images: A Study In Copper

Critique Verses Criticism   136
    Firestorm

Finding a Good Support System   139
    Poppies

The Art of Gratitude   142
    Windows

As This Book Comes to an End…   146

Information and Websites of Interest   150

Index of Quilts   151

Introduction

I love being an artist. I love the art form of quilting and the work I am able to create. I love to work with people. Besides art, my other passion is to travel. I am very blessed in my life to combine all my loves into a single profession, the calling of being a quilt teacher.

While nature is the primary influence for much of my artwork, nothing inspires me on a personal level more than my students. My students are a joy. I may be the teacher in class, but what I learn from them in return is invaluable. They motivate and stimulate me. They encourage me with kind words when I need to hear them most. Their enthusiasm inspires my enthusiasm. Their creativity stirs my creativity. My give-and-take connection with my students is a beautiful and nourishing relationship. I've developed and maintained many wonderful friendships with my students all over the world.

Over the years, my students have expressed an interest in my life, the symbolism behind my quilts and the personal stories discussed in my lectures. They urged me to write my thoughts and experiences on paper. Because of their encouragement, *Nurture Your Creative Spirit* was born.

After working in various art mediums, I found my niche in quilting. Although told from a quilter's point of view, the lessons in *Nurture Your Creative Spirit* pertain to all art forms. I write about the wisdoms I learned from quilting, traits of creative people and the significances of my quilts. I discuss inspiration, how emotions affect our artistic productivity and numerous subjects that relate to all manner of art.

Passages of the Spirit (Detail)

Nurture Your Creative Spirit is a labor of love for me; it rewards with feelings of joy and fulfillment. Writing this book has been a dear learning experience, giving me a chance for introspection and realizing knowledge of self. The following pages allow me the opportunity to share my knowledge and insights with you.

I reached deep within my heart and soul to write *Nurture Your Creative Spirit*. When you work from the heart and soul in any art form, whatever is in you, *everything* that is in you, emerges. As with my quilts, some of my most personal thoughts and spiritual feelings surface in these pages. In some passages throughout the book, I talk about my spiritual insights and mention "God," the spiritual deity in my life. Spirituality is deeply personal and we live in an ecumenical society with diverse forms of worship. As you come to these passages, please substitute the deity of your faith or "higher being" or "universe."

I pray that you see yourself in these pages. As you read *Nurture Your Creative Spirit*, give thought to your own experiences. What can you learn about yourself and your art? How have you blossomed over the years? What stories and knowledge can you share with others?

As you consider your own artistic journey, it is my hope that *Nurture Your Creative Spirit* will enable you to flourish creatively, filling you with inspiration, insight, and pleasure.

With love,

Nikki

Promise of Spring (Detail)

The Improbable Quilter

When people view my quilts, one of my most frequently asked questions is, "How long did it take you to make this quilt?" I always smile to myself. Of course, the answer they are expecting is "six months" or "a year." The correct answer is forty plus years.

It is true that every craft and art form I've explored throughout my life influenced my work today. Equally true, my life experiences and changing temperament over the years played a significant role in the way I interpret elements and objects as well. My artistic style has changed. As a young woman, my attitudes and mind-set were more rigid and perfectionistic. My artistry reflected those viewpoints. Everything had to be perfect and realistic. My ability to create with freedom and imagination was limited. As a mature woman, I've mellowed. I am more tolerant and open-minded. My visual style has transformed into one that is more abstract, self-revealing and expressionistic. I am open to all possibilities when I create. My imagination no longer has boundaries.

My art, as yours, is a journey that takes years, perhaps a lifetime. It is the journey and the process, not the final destination that is ultimately important. I've come to realize that life's experiences and attitudes guide one's direction and course. Being aware of the twists, turns and detours on your path may enable you to better understand yourself and the effects these diversions have on your art.

The earliest recollections of my creative endeavors began ages ago as a young child. In kindergarten, I lived to finger paint. It was the highlight of my entire school year. I can remember getting completely involved in the creative process. I dearly loved freely expressing myself with the messy paints and glossy paper. I hated to stop when the teacher said it was time to move on to another activity.

On the other hand, seventh grade challenged my creativity. I had to take a Home Economics course. All the girls did. Personally, I would have preferred to learn Industrial Arts, but girls were not allowed to participate in the boys' class; it just wasn't offered to girls at that time. Of course, boys did not take Home Economics either. As I suspect it to be true for many other working women, it would have been a blessing to have a husband who could sew a button on his shirt and be able to cook an occasional meal other than boiled hot dogs. Luckily, it's different these days. Sometimes the old ways aren't necessarily better.

Anyway, as part of the Home Economics curriculum, we learned to sew…or at least some of us did. My project, a pink-flowered housecoat, was dreadful. I hated every minute of the sewing process and swore I'd never sew again. In retrospect and knowing what I do now, I think it was because I couldn't follow the rules for sewing. It wasn't fun and my heart wasn't in it.

I remember the inspiration I felt as a young teen, gazing at the beautiful stained glass windows in our church. I dreamt of becoming an artist, painting religious art like those windows. Today, I create art filled with spirituality, not as a traditional painter, but in a different medium—quilting. Our dreams do come true, not always as we want or how we envision, but as God envisions.

In 1968, at the tender age of nineteen, I married my husband, Denny. After our daughter was born in 1971 and our son in 1975, I became a stay-at-home mom. I became more involved with arts and crafts, at first to relieve the stress of everyday childcare, then as a wonderful way to retreat into my own quiet world.

Little did I realize over the next four decades, I would delve into many different mediums in crafts and the fine arts. I would work in oils, watercolors, sculpture and with all manner of crafts. With the exception of a few beginning lessons in painting at a local craft shop in the early 1970s, and several classes in my early years of quilting, all my art forms are self-taught. In my twenties, I learned to paint, first with oil, then watercolor. I painted murals, flowers, landscapes, portraits of my children, myself, parents, and sister and brother-in-law. I also trained myself how to sculpt with clay.

I was happy in my insulated, creative world, where it was private and quiet. That all ended in 1981. My mother, Mary, became ill and quickly was diagnosed with pancreatic cancer. She died within a few months. Losing heart after her passing, my father died the following year. After my parents were gone, I was devastated. I lost all will and desire to create. I occasionally played at crafts, but was unable to focus on anything serious.

Ten years later in 1991, my sister, Augustine Ellis, asked me to take a beginning quilting class with her. The woman who planned to accompany her had to cancel. I promptly said "No" to my sister. No way was I going to a sewing class. I hated to sew. Undaunted, she persisted until I finally relented and agreed to go with her and give it a try. I had to placate her somehow. My sister's family and ours have lived next door to

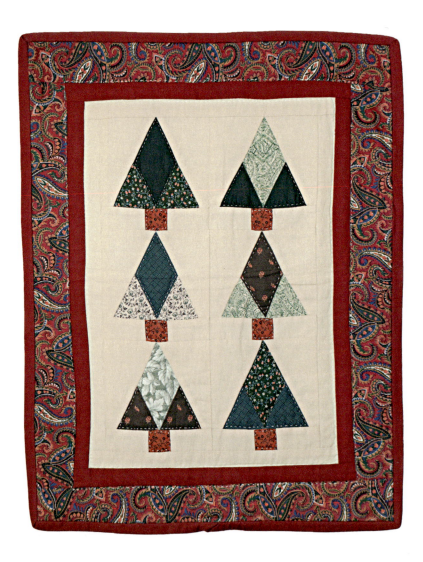

each other since 1983.

From the moment I started my beginning class, I quickly became excited and enamored with the exquisite art of quiltmaking. I felt my desire to create begin to revive. That class was the turning point, the end of the creative hiatus that began with my parents' deaths. I've been obsessed with quilting and collecting fabric since that day. Unlike my housecoat project in junior high school, this type of sewing was interesting, fun and gave me the opportunity to be creative.

The quilt project in my beginning class was a pre-made kit. The design was comprised of six blocks… each block containing a triangular-shaped evergreen tree. The quilt was hand-pieced and hand-quilted. Even though I was proud of my first quilt at

My First Quilt (18˝ × 22½˝): A kit supplied by the quilt shop, this piece was hand-pieced and hand-quilted.

14   Nurture Your Creative Spirit

the time, the adjective "pitiful" describes it accurately. I still include that quilt in my trunk shows to illustrate how far one can progress with time and persistence.

After completing my beginner's quilt, I started working with other traditional patterns and ideas, but would change them as much as I could to make them my own. In all my artistic undertakings, I've never been content to follow another person's design or replicate anything that someone else has done. I must do my own thing. I love individuality and uniqueness in everything in life, no matter what it may be. I always strive to create original artwork and follow my own artistic path.

I felt a wonderful sense of satisfaction as I managed to explore my newfound art form and complete each new project, especially as a novice who knew little about sewing. Who could have ever guessed that quilting (and sewing) would become my career and play such a massive part in my life? Never in a million years would I have dreamt of such a thing.

My artistic course continues with each passing day. Though visual art is my love, writing this book is part of my creative odyssey as well. Writing about my journey and its detours has brought about a lot of introspection and enlightenment. I hope to share some of the lessons I've learned with you. I also hope you will take time to contemplate your own personal artistic passage as you read this book. The knowledge you glean will open a whole new world of understanding for you.

Traits That Nurture Creativity

Reflecting on my growth, not only since I started to quilt, but with all art mediums and creative endeavors in my life since kindergarten, I realize there are definite characteristics or traits that contribute to, enhance and nurture my art. Courage, persistence, determination, curiosity, passion, flexibility, sharing, faith in myself and my work, and keeping a sense of humor, among others, are instrumental in growing, not only in art but in everyday life as well. These lessons became apparent with each quilt I made or in some cases, struggled to finish.

Breaking Point (Detail)

Determination

My husband, Denny, will tell you I've always possessed the trait of determination. Actually, he may say stubbornness. He uses both words to describe me. But my determination level was put to the test with my first original quilt design.

That first design was a tree blowing wildly in the throes of a violent spring thunderstorm. A pear tree growing in the front yard of our home was the inspiration. The tree's fight for survival in that terrible storm touched me deeply, and its struggle matched my emotional state at the time. Our family

Breaking Point (Details, pages 17 and 18. Full view on page 49; 46½″ × 29″): The idea for my quilt, *Breaking Point*, was born in 1994 while our family was suffering through some very stressful times. We were dealing with my husband, Denny's, diagnosis and bout with kidney cancer, his mother's heart disease and death, health issues with our beloved pet Yorkshire terrier and the frustrating trials and tribulations of dealing with teenage children. I felt I might snap if even one more disastrous event happened to us. I was inspired to make *Breaking Point* as I watched the violent winds of a spring storm batter and bend the branches of a beautiful tree in our front yard. I felt at one with that tree. As the tree, I also was at my breaking point.

The focal tree in the quilt symbolizes each of us as individuals and the blowing winds and rain are the inevitable storms of life we all must endure. One way to survive is to be flexible, to bend and ride out the storm rather than fight against it. This quilt relates to the stresses all people face at one time or another in their lives, especially those in middle age who must deal with coinciding, challenging issues such as aging parents, teens and young adult children and sometimes life-threatening disease.

Ironically, as I was sewing this quilt during the summer, yet another violent thunderstorm toppled a major section of that tree. The tree remained sturdy until 2010, when it finally succumbed to fire blight disease. It was heartbreaking to take down the tree. It was, and still is, my symbol of endurance in the face of life's storms.

was dealing with many personal storms of our own, including my husband's diagnosis of kidney cancer. Making this quilt would help me heal. I already knew the title. I would call it *Breaking Point*.

Even though I was a novice quilter with no sewing experience, I decided to go forward and create this healing quilt with over two hundred pieces…all of them curves. I was so naïve. It just never occurred to me this would be a problem; that is, until the day I started to piece together the first two patches. Not only wouldn't the patches lay flat, I figured I'd be about a hundred years old before I finally finished the darn thing. There had to be an easier way. The desire to find a better technique challenged me to be creative.

So, using trial and error methods, I grabbed some freezer paper and started to experiment with all the possibilities and ideas that popped into my mind, whether inspired or inane.

Lightning Strikes Twice (46½˝ × 29˝): *Breaking Point* proved to be a very healing quilt for me, made after my husband's bout with cancer. This image is the symbolic back art on the quilt. Cancer has affected my family twice. Cancer claimed my mother, Mary, in 1981. Fortunately, my husband's surgery for cancer was successful and he is in excellent health today. The two lightning bolts symbolize the disease that struck twice…my Mom and my husband.

I positioned two cafeteria tables so they were parallel about four feet apart, then removed the long glass panel out of our storm door and laid it on top of the two tables, spanning the gap. I put a lamp on the floor beneath the glass, creating a huge light table. I taped the *Breaking Point* pattern to the underside of the glass.

From the top side, I could easily see the seam lines of the pattern. I traced a couple of templates onto freezer paper, cut them apart and fused each template to the right side of my chosen fabric. I left a fabric seam allowance on all edges of the patch.

I decided that rather than easing and stitching the right sides of the patches together for curved templates, it was easier to work in sequence and overlap them. I could lay the first patch flat, then using the freezer paper template edge as a guideline, turn under the seam allowance along the adjoining edge of the second patch. Using the makeshift light table, I was able to see the pattern seam line and could position the second patch to overlap the seam allowance of the first patch.

The lessons came quickly. The first thing I learned, besides a vocabulary of new words, was that I needed to clip the "valleys" of concave curves or the fabric wouldn't turn under to the back. The second fast lesson was that fabric cut unevenly and joined in all different directions will warp and unmercifully stretch out of shape. I realized I needed a foundation fabric to hold the patches flat and in place. With no clue about what to use, I chose a densely-woven, white cotton fabric. Luckily, for a small quilt like *Breaking Point,* it worked fine. After *Breaking Point*, I began to use a non-woven, sew-in stabilizer in a medium weight as the foundation for my quilts. These washable, sew-in stabilizers (not interfacings) are normally available at fabric stores and are a poly/rayon blend. Today, I would use the white cotton fabric as a foundation only for wearable art projects because the cotton provides a better drape.

Eventually, I finished *Breaking Point* and felt proud of my accomplishment. I wanted to share my triumph and new work with others. As a novice quilter, I loved reading *Quilter's Newsletter Magazine.* I particularly enjoyed reading a regular feature in the magazine, "Quilting Bee." The magazine invited readers of all skill levels to submit quilts and their stories for publication. I decided to submit my story and an image of

Breaking Point. After all, what did I have to lose? Nothing. The worst that could happen is the magazine would say "No."

Three months later, I received an acceptance to publish the image. To say I was thrilled is an understatement. I filled out the required permission-to-publish contract. One question in the contract asked if there was a pattern available for this original work. I responded "Yes." "Do you want to know how I did the curves?" I innocently inquired since I hadn't used conventional techniques. Well, I did hear back and yes, they *did* want to know. "Write an article," the editor told me. Of course, I would!

It finally dawned on me with some dismay I couldn't tell my readers to take down their storm doors and straddle them on cafeteria tables. It was back to the drawing board... and more trial and error. Ultimately, with more patience and determination, I honed and perfected my curved piecing technique without the makeshift light table, using only freezer paper, foundation and sequential piecing. The new technique I developed for the article is the same one I teach today. *Quilter's Newsletter Magazine* published the article titled "Mosaic Applique" and the image of *Breaking Point* and its story in the October 1996 issue. Until then I was teaching sporadically on a local level. With the publication of my article, I began receiving invitations to speak and teach all over the country. Thus began my career as a quilting instructor.

So what did I learn from *Breaking Point*? I discovered when something does go wrong and mistakes happen, I must stay optimistic and not get discouraged or consider it a personal failure. I learned to keep an open mind and consider every possibility, no matter how bizarre, for a solution. I constantly ask myself "What if" when I create. For instance, "What if I substitute another color?" or "What if I change the design or perspective?" or maybe, "What happens if I try using another method?" Asking "What if" while you work on a project benefits you by boosting your creativity, imagination, flexibility and curiosity.

I acquired a few other new mantras as well, among them: "Be flexible," "Keep it simple" and "Do whatever it takes to make something work." Trial and error is a good teacher. Knowing what is not successful is just as important as knowing what is.

At times when we work, we have to find a solution out of necessity or must deal with limitations or restrictions that are out of our control. These challenges dare us to think creatively. The seemingly impossible is possible if you want it passionately enough. I knew I could succeed if I kept a good outlook, stayed focused and put my heart into my work. I wouldn't give up and found out just how obstinate I can be when I am intent on my art. As I said, Denny calls me stubborn, but I laugh and tell him it's determination.

Determination is an essential quality and is key to any major accomplishment in one's life. It is important in quilting as well. Have conviction to tackle problems head-on with imaginative solutions and ideas. If you are adamant that you want to achieve results for a project, you will find a way to do it. As the old cliché goes, "Where there's a will, there's a way." I find this old saying is often true.

Determination is a state of mind, and it requires a resolute attitude, a confident approach to a situation and a positive intention. Most likely you will succeed if you tell yourself, "*I can* do this. I *will* prevail." If your outlook is half-hearted, chances are good you won't succeed. You will produce mediocre work if you embark on a project without drive, full commitment and enthusiasm.

One must maintain a strong desire to succeed and carry out what may seem to be a difficult or even impossible task. Perhaps it may be a problem that you don't have a clue how to tackle. Even so, jump in and begin working on the project. Be confident, think optimistically and expect to succeed. The answers will come as you work.

Determination requires a lot of effort and strength of will and is not an easy trait to sustain, especially when you are having difficulties with the project, feeling tired, depressed or physically limited. During those times, do as much as you are able, but stay committed to your intent.

Persistence

Another important trait of creative people is to be persistent. Persistence is a close cousin to determination, but with a difference. Determination is the intention to accomplish something. Persistence is the dogged tenacity to stick with it for the long term.

Unfortunately, some people expect instant success and become frustrated and disillusioned when they hit a roadblock. At the first sign of trouble, they are easily defeated, give up and are unable to maintain the commitment it takes to tackle the difficulty and see it through.

We must remember the wonderful gift of creativity belongs to all of us. Everyone possesses it. But creativity, and all the answers to whatever problem we are trying to

Fire and Ice (44˝ × 45˝): My second original quilt, *Fire and Ice*, is a study in colors and incorporating straight and curved shapes. The flaming, vivid reds, yellows and oranges of fire are in direct contrast to the jagged, icy blues, grays and lavenders of winter. The inspiration for this quilt was a comforting fire in our fireplace during a cold winter's night.

Fire and Ice represents my persistence. I managed to finish *Breaking Point* using two cafeteria tables and a storm door as a makeshift light box. Could I do it again, this time with my newly honed method? Absolutely. I had no trouble constructing *Fire and Ice* with my new construction technique. On a whim, I submitted the quilt into the *Pennsylvania National Quilt Extravaganza* (Mancuso Show Management), where it won my very first award, "Best Amateur Entry."

solve in our art project, don't always come easily. Possible solutions exist; we have to search for them. Be clever. Inventive. Ingenious. It's been said if you can dream or envision it, you can do it. The key to success is persistence.

Quitting is seldom an option for me. I complete most of what I start, usually one project at a time. I focus on it until it is finished. There are times, especially with class designs or testing out a new technique idea, I deliberately know in advance I won't finish. I learn the concept or technique and move on, using it in another work that is important to me. I save the original as a reference.

Choosing colors and fabric patches for a quilt top is my favorite aspect of quilting. Although I complete all my quilts myself, I could be totally content creating only quilt tops. I love the challenge and the process of choosing the colors and blending them to complete the vision I see in my imagination. It is not uncommon for me to take up to forty-five minutes or an hour to hunt through my fabrics for a single patch. I have a pretty good idea in my mind of what material I have in my stash and will search until I find the exact one I need, the colors the quilt is calling out for. I am obstinately persistent when choosing the right patch for a quilt top.

Aftermath: The row of partially melted icicles on the back of *Fire and Ice* is the hanging sleeve. The theme represents the aftermath of fire and ice: the embers and melting icicles.

My secret to staying persistent is to see the predicament as a personal challenge. And I do love a challenge. Whether spending hours working puzzles in the newspaper, looking for the three cent mistake in my checkbook or making a quilt, my reaction is the same: The more something seems impossible to accomplish, the more I dig in my heels and am adamant to figure it out. I don't give up easily.

There will be times you come to an impasse, uncertain what to do or how to do it. You may have to set your quilt aside for a while before you renew your efforts. Don't give up. Let the problem simmer on the back burner of your mind and come back to it later. A short break may be just the ticket to offer you a fresh look and a new solution.

There is a saying: If your mind is stuck, work with your hands. Instead of fretting about the standstill in your project, switch off the mental gears causing the stress. Use your hands by substituting other temporary, mind-freeing physical outlets such as working in the garden, cooking or playing with an unrelated, fun craft for a change of scenery. These activities relax the mind. In effect, you are putting emotional distance between you and the difficulty.

As an alternative suggestion, you might try to construct a very simple quilt block or similar easy-to-do design. Working on a stress-free pattern that you are comfortable with helps to boost your self-confidence. Sometimes you just need to prove something to yourself. "I **can** do this well. I **am** a

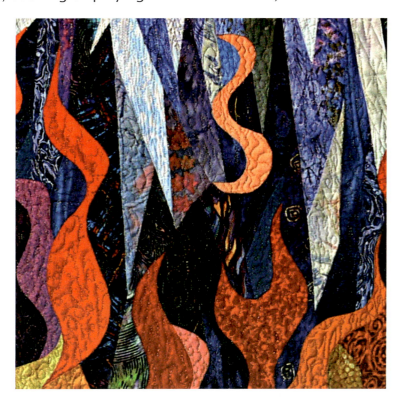

Fire and Ice (Detail)

Traits That Nurture Creativity

good quilter." Then, when you turn your attention back to the wayward design or problem quilt, you will be mentally refreshed with more confidence and determination.

There have been occasions when I started a work and didn't complete it until years later. At the time, I didn't have the techniques, the knowledge or the right materials to make the piece into what it was destined to be.

If all else fails, there may be a point when it is necessary to quit and cut your losses. Evaluate your task. Perhaps you have taken the quilt as far as it can go. A dubious pursuit is not worth the struggle if you are utterly frustrated and feel strongly about stopping. Unfinished work does not imply failure. Every effort produces a result. Whether that result is considered an achievement or a disappointment depends only on your judgment call. If you decide to abandon your endeavor, take a moment to reflect. Did you learn anything while working on it? Maybe the project's sole purpose was to teach a lesson, not to be finished. With this insight, you'll know the time and energy spent was not wasted.

However, if it is a worthy venture, exhaust all the avenues first. Don't give up easily or too soon. Do not let quitting become a habit. Be persistent when things don't go smoothly. Keep on working until the problem is resolved.

With a self-confident and optimistic outlook you cannot fail. You can only learn and improve. All of the great theories, inventions and works of art we enjoy now, things that were made with human hands, minds and spirit, did not come into being without determination, persistence, heartbreak and the challenge of many setbacks.

Humor

Humor is a positive trait that nurtures and promotes creativity. If you keep an upbeat attitude looking at the lighter side of life, the happier you'll be. The happier you are, the more creative you'll be. From personal experience, I know my productivity increases when I am feeling lighthearted.

Feelin' Groovy: It is not the front of *Blacklick Pond: Reflections at Twilight* that represents humor, but the back art, *Feelin' Groovy*. Blacklick Pond is full of life: animals, flowers, birds, vegetation, insects, fish and frogs…thousands of frogs! I love to listen to the frogs croaking. Doesn't this little guy look like he's smiling and happily guilty as though he just snatched the last dragonfly? By the way, this quilt does have a hanging sleeve. The sleeve is part of the patchwork at the top.

Keep a sense of humor in your work rather than taking yourself too seriously. Humor helps you keep life in perspective and retain an optimistic viewpoint. Seldom does everything in life come easily or go smoothly as planned. You might as well look for the whimsy in situations to keep your sanity and peace of mind.

One way I stay upbeat is by being adaptable. I try not to focus on a specific outcome or result in my work. I anticipate and welcome the unexpected results that sometimes happen, whether strange or even bizarre. Even though the final outcome may not be what is originally intended, remember creativity is all about uniqueness, perspective and especially finding delight in your work.

Slow down. Connect with the simple things in life. Take time to observe the natural world around you. Be amused and smile at the little pleasures you see, hear, smell and feel.

Blacklick Pond: Reflections at Twilight (Detail shown; full size 53˝ × 53˝): My home is near Blacklick Woods, one of the beautiful metro parks surrounding the city of Columbus, Ohio. I often retreat into the woods to enjoy and draw upon the peace and solitude that enhances creativity. Within the park is a quiet secluded pond, the inspiration for *Blacklick Pond: Reflections at Twilight.* This quilt represents the season of summer—busy, vibrant and teeming with life. In summer, the pond flourishes with raucous, gleeful song and lush colors.

I believe we mortals also go through seasonal passages. In the summer of our lives, we are as the season—busily occupied, happy and optimistic. I've tried to portray those moods. In my quilt, there is more in life than we can know or see, thus the continuance of the quilt after the black borders. The uneven sides represent detours in life's journey we all face.

Blacklick Pond: Reflections at Twilight is the third original quilt I designed. So enamored by this beautiful spot in the park, I decided to do a series of four "pond" quilts, one for each season of the year.

For example, when I'm beachcombing at the seashore I love to sit and watch the sandpipers. They run back and forth along the edge of the water, dodging the crashing waves to feed on creatures in the sand. I can't help but smile when I watch them run, their little legs moving a mile a minute. It's uncanny how they avoid the water. And they manage to do it much better than I. I always misjudge the approaching wave and get soaked to the knees.

While watching the sandpipers, I love to sit and quietly listen to the relentless and eternal sound of the ocean waves crashing on shore or feel the caress of the ocean's breezes on my face or rejoice in the smell of the salty air. I know it's easy to stay upbeat at the seashore, but the same joys are also in your backyard. The breezes you feel are just as caressing and the birds as entertaining as those on the beach. The

Maintaining humor allows you to stay relaxed in mind, body and spirit. Lightheartedness allows you to retain the playfulness and spontaneity in your creativity. Work continues to be enjoyable. Without maintaining a sense of humor, you may become stressed and anxious, and possibly, it will show in your work. Also, staying cheerful helps you keep close friends. People prefer to be around someone who smiles and enjoys what they do rather than be with a grouch. So, be optimistic and let your work be fun.

sounds of the crickets, rustling leaves or the joyous colors of the sunrises and sunsets are there as well if you take the time to notice. We are so involved with the busyness in our lives we seldom observe, smile and be amused and grateful for the simple joys right before our eyes. Yet being content and positive is critical for our creative health as well as our physical and spiritual well-being.

Flexibility

Flexibility is an absolute must for the innovative person. One must be open-minded and objective to be imaginative. Creativity simply cannot grow if one is rigid. However, some people resist and dislike change; they are set in their ways. They prefer life to be predictable and keep a routine. But change keeps things fresh and interesting. The world around us is constantly evolving. In art, as in life, if you choose routine you stay in a rut and do not grow.

Finding inspiration is much easier when you are open and receptive to new ideas. One of the mantra lessons I learned from *Breaking Point* is "Do whatever it takes to make it work." I think this mantra is a metaphor and holds true not only for quiltmaking, but relates to dealing with life's issues as well. In both life and quilting, it is counterproductive to stay stubbornly fixed to specific thoughts when the outcomes are unsuccessful. Instead, consider all the possibilities, angles and perspectives.

To resolve setbacks that arise in your quilting and design work, be adaptable

The inspiration for *Against All Odds*.

in making choices and look for potential solutions. Give thought to every possibility even if you are uncertain if it will work or you are unsure how to tackle the how-to construction issues. Look at the situation from every angle and viewpoint. Consider unusual choices of color. You might ask a trusted friend for an opinion. Brainstorm with her or him about potential solutions to the problem. Constructive feedback from another is invaluable to an artist.

A possible answer to your quilting or design dilemma may involve turning your quilt around or upside down, changing the perspective (near or far) or substituting an unlikely color...one that you never dreamt would work. Never limit your palette to only colors you like. All colors, the dull, yucky and yes, even the ones you hate are useful and necessary. They have a place in the world and in your work.

Flexible people never stay rooted to an original idea if the design doesn't want to work. You must let the quilt blossom and take on a life of its own. Almost without exception, the result is better than your original vision.

Quilts can tell you what they want to be. They will guide you to completion. Often, I wonder if they are a living, breathing entity. At least it seems that way. Have you ever

Against All Odds (62½˝ × 85˝): I am inspired by trees in the western United States that seem to defy gravity and reason and grow out of bare rock, their root tips seeking nourishment from an unseen source. Though twisted and misformed, they are beautiful creations. Against all odds, these trees manage to persevere and even thrive in harsh elements. But nature is patient and the trees are strong and resilient. Over time, the trees will break apart the rock.

I've always admired subtle comparisons between humans and trees and our existence together on this earth. I dedicated this quilt to people who struggle with life's burdens in their daily lives but somehow manage to hang on by sheer will and even flourish.

The sky was created by layering multiple colors of polyester sheer organza. The leaves and tree were constructed using felting techniques to mesh cotton fabrics, silks, raw wool and raw silk fibers, polyester sheer organza, cheesecloth and threads. My topstitch technique, using cotton fabrics for the rocks, completed *Against All Odds.*

been working happily on a quilt, only to come to a complete standstill? No matter what you do or how much you try to go forward, you cannot. It's as if you are hitting against a brick wall. In a moment of inspiration (or desperation), you change from your original idea and start working with new thoughts. Amazingly, the progress on

Against All Odds (Detail)

the quilt will start to flow again as it should. This scenario has happened to me again and again. Coincidence? I don't think so.

It is my belief God talks to us and makes Himself heard through the words and actions of others. I believe the inspirations and ideas we receive for quilts, or any other creative art form, come from the Divine. We are channels through which the Divine flows. Each quilt is a treasure and has a purpose for being, whether destined for exhibition in a museum or as a source of comfort to be cherished by a child.

Red Sky at Night (29˝ × 29˝)

The only way these artistic inspirations can be born into the world is through our hands. As instruments, it is our job to let them flow through us and stay out of the way. Let the quilt become what it is supposed to be. You will know. When you are on the right path, the work progresses and flows smoothly like the current of a river. When you are not on the right path, the flow blocks... just like a dam. Aspire to be open to new ideas while you are working. Do not stay devotedly focused on your initial idea if your work progress stops flowing or you feel you are fighting to make the quilt work.

My quilt *Against All Odds* is a good example of blocked flow. In the beginning, I planned to create the struggling tree and its leaves using innovative felting techniques and piece the rocks and sky with cotton fabrics using my usual topstitch construction method. I finished the tree and leaves quickly and was thrilled with the results. The sky, however, was a pain. No matter which fabrics or colors used, I couldn't achieve good results or get the necessary value or color contrast I knew the quilt should have. I fussed with the sky for months. Finally, at a loss, I sat down and tried to consider what else I could possibly do.

I thought about a small sample quilt I had experimented with earlier containing polyester sheer organza fabrics, titled *Red Sky at Night*. I utilized multiple colors and layers of the sheers to create a vibrant sunset scene. Although *Against All Odds* was shaping up to be a large quilt, I wondered if that same sheer layering technique would work for the sky. Feeling there was nothing to lose by trying, I set about cutting the sheers for the sky.

Unbelievably, I completed the entire sky section of *Against All Odds* in a three short days. I was amazed how much the vibrant colors of the sheer organza fabrics added to the visual impact. The sky contrasted beautifully against the rocks and trees. I'm sure there was no better choice for this quilt. From that point forward the work progressed rapidly. Everything, including me, was flowing again.

Against All Odds includes another example of flexibility as well. During the construction phase, I intended to position the felted tree shape completely reversed from how it is now. While placing the tree on the quilt top, I wondered, "What if?" Then, I flipped the tree upside down. The limbs I fashioned as roots are now the tree branches in the sky... and the twisted branches I formed are now the roots. I discovered I liked the tree much better this way. The original branches were better suited as the sprawling, curvy roots growing into the rocks. The original roots made beautiful branches and fit well on the sky section. The moral of the story is do not stay "rooted" to the initial idea; let the quilt grow, and allow yourself to grow along with it.

Against All Odds isn't the only quilt that taught me to be flexible. *Tears on Blacklick Pond* taught me the same hard lesson in 1996. *"Tears"* was my fourth innovative quilt and the second in my "pond" series. I easily designed and constructed the quilt top. Problems came when I decided to include back art. Since the quilt depicted an autumn scene with fallen leaves, I thought it would be fitting to design a tree, in silhouette with bare branches, on the back of the quilt. In my stash, I found a pretty red-orange leaf fabric for the background. This fabric was the perfect choice for a fall-themed quilt. I had just enough material for the back, or so I thought.

Notice the asymmetrical shape of *Tears on Blacklick Pond* (page 38.) To design the back art, I first had to start with boundaries; I needed to draw the shape of the completed quilt top hanging on my design wall. I tried to decide what would be the easiest way to transfer the perimeter lines of the quilt to my enlarged drawing paper. The simplest approach I could think of was to position and secure the drawing paper to the quilt top, covering its front surface, then sketch the approximate perimeter lines. That is exactly what I did.

I drafted and pieced the back art. There were few fabrics in the design, only the black fabrics for the silhouette and the red leaf fabric for the background. When I finished piecing, I had only a smidgen of

Tears on Blacklick Pond (Detail)

the red fabric left. I prepared to sandwich the back art, batting and the quilt top.

Probably, most of you have guessed already what I did wrong. I forgot to reverse my pattern before I pieced it. Because the perimeter was asymmetrical and different lengths on every side, the back art did not match up with the quilt top. It was short in several places and I had no more red leaf fabric.

It is an understatement to say I was furious for my lack of foresight. After venting my anger for 15 minutes, I sat down in a chair across from my design wall and just stared at my problem child. What to do now?

After some thought, I realized if I added strips of another material to extend the quilt back, it would be large enough to match the quilt top. I sliced off three sides of the quilt back and sewed strips of fabric to the center section. Then I reattached the corresponding cut sections to the new strips. I opted for turquoise blue for the extension fabric for several reasons. First, it is the complementary color of red-orange,

There are many analogies between quilting and life. In both, one may follow a pattern as a path to reach an objective. Or, a person may create or live in a spontaneous manner to achieve his or her aim. In either case, whether working on a quilt or a life goal, each day brings new setbacks and challenges. Usually, the way one handles challenges during the art-making process parallels how one copes with life's obstacles. I believe the answer in both instances is staying calm, flexible and open-minded. Consider all options and possibilities, even the most unlikely, as prospective solutions to the problems we encounter on a daily basis.

Tears on Blacklick Pond (60˝ × 58˝): The fall season at Blacklick Woods Metro Park in Reynoldsburg, Ohio is the inspiration for my quilt, *Tears on Blacklick Pond*. The floating autumn leaves are beautiful and colorful at secluded Blacklick Pond. I delight in these leaves drifting around me, swirling in the breeze. Yet this is a bittersweet time. The leaves are tears and their fall signals the death of the season. As with *Blacklick Pond: Reflections at Twilight*, the continuance of the quilt after the inner black borders represents that there is life again after death. The uneven sides depict the uncertainty of our lives.

Silhouette: Back art on my quilt *Tears on Blacklick Pond*. While the front surface of the quilt features the beauty of the autumn leaves, the back focuses on the tree itself. It remains bare and dormant until spring. The red background represents the fallen leaves and the turquoise blue strips symbolize the water of Blacklick Pond. Creating the back art for this quilt taught me the lesson of flexibility.

so there would be a pleasing contrast and visual interest. Secondly, I could write my quilt's artist's statement to say I chose the blue fabric intentionally and it symbolizes the water in the pond on the front of the quilt, thus covering up my slip. "No one needs to know," I thought with injured pride.

After some reflection, I decided I could use this quilt as an example to illustrate an important point about making mistakes. Now at my lectures and in class, I freely tell my audience about the blunders I make. We all err. What is important here is not giving up, getting angry or trying to do things perfectly, but staying flexible and searching for ways to correct the situation. Never fret about making errors. They stretch your imagination and inventiveness. If you are not making mistakes, you are not growing to your potential.

Actually, my oversight ended up being a blessing. The back art on *"Tears"* turned out much better visually and artistically (which I find is often the case) than if I had kept the original design.

Patience

I received the inspiration for *Portrait of My Soul* during an evening church service. The priest assigned to our church at the time often gave dry sermons and no matter how hard I tried to pay attention, I would lose interest and start daydreaming. The talk on this particular day was no different from some of the others. As my mind drifted, I clearly visualized an image that I felt portrayed my spirit. I perceived my spirit as a sunburst of energy, swirling and constantly moving, vibrating, almost flickering. The

Portrait of My Soul (Details, pages 41 and 42; full size 65˝ x 65˝): I conceived the idea and inspiration for this quilt during a church service. Instead of paying attention to the sermon, my mind wandered. I clearly visualized an image I feel portrays my spirit. The motion and colors in *Portrait of My Soul* are symbolic, representing my energy and emotions.

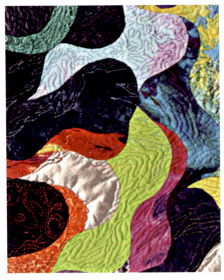
vivid, colorful flame-like shapes were symbolic and depicted the emotions that affect me. I saw my anxieties and insecurities intermixed with my joys and virtues. The color red represented love and passion; purple symbolized spirituality and sorrow; blue, serenity; yellow, joy; gray indicated my fear and anxiety; etc. The gold color represented God. The darkness surrounding my spirit symbolized the world. The name for my new quilt was obvious: *Portrait of My Soul*.

Enthralled by the inspirational idea for a new quilt but ignoring the fact Denny and I were sitting only three pews back from the priest, I grabbed a ballpoint pen from my husband's pocket and the closest piece of paper, which happened to be a church bulletin. Afraid I'd forget the details, I started to sketch my vision on the back of the bulletin.

I must have awakened Denny when I snatched his pen because he turned and asked me what I was doing. I told him I was drawing an idea for a quilt, to which he replied, "I can't take you anywhere." He's probably right. I can find designs and ideas for quilting almost everywhere I go. But I wasn't in the mood to listen to him and while not remembering my exact words, I basically told him I was having a special moment and he should leave me alone and go back to sleep.

I started designing *Portrait of My Soul* the next morning. Construction of the quilt top was quick, easy and flawless. I completed the quilt top exactly how I visualized it that evening in church. Quilting it was another story. *Portrait of My Soul* taught me several lessons, among them patience and the folly of perfectionism.

By this time in my new career, I'd entered lots of high-level quilt competitions. Unbelievably for a sewing novice, I won quite a few awards. I set the standards high for myself and, always a perfectionist, demanded nothing short of excellence in my work.

During the quilting process, I often felt my free-motion stitching didn't measure up to my standards. I tore out stitches and quilted over the same areas time after time until I was certain my quilting was perfect enough to enter into competition. I swear, some days I ripped out more stitches than I put in. I was totally stressed, frustrated, hating every moment of the quilting process and by now,  hating the quilt too. Nothing helped. Not even the hunk of chocolate or glass of wine that usually gets me through the rough times when I have thread tension issues with my free-motion quilting.

I went to visit and seek advice from my sewing machine dealer, Susan Hart. I love her to pieces, even more than a quilter loves a newfound fabric shop. Susan ranks among the top women on my all-time favorite people list. She helped me get my start in quilting and made sure I had a good machine when I couldn't afford one. She has guided me many times and in many ways over the years.

Portrait of My Soul: Detail of free-motion machine stitching from *Portrait of My Soul*. During the time of construction, I felt my work was short of perfection.

Quilting this work taught me another valuable lesson. Metallic thread became popular to use for the quilting process when I was a novice. Enamored with glitzy thread, I used it to quilt entire projects. Yet, I was disappointed with the results. I didn't understand why my stitching lacked pizazz. Later, I realized it was because I used the same type of thread for the total surface. There was no contrast or variety. Once I offset the shiny metallic strands with matte thread, and the bright colors with quiet, dark ones, my stitching came alive. I learned as with life, being in balance pertains to thread as well.

I told Susan the problems I was having quilting my new quilt. She must have guessed right away that it was my perfectionism holding me back because she said to me, "Whom are you doing this quilt for? Yourself or the judges?" Her words prodded me to think. What were my true motives? It occurred to me I was caught up in ego. My desire for recognition and perfection was so strong, I was losing sight of the joy of creating and sharing my inspiration with others. After that insightful conversation with Susan, I was able to finish that quilt in a few short days…relieved, happy and a lot wiser.

What did I learn from *Portrait of My Soul*? I came to understand how vital it is to be patient with myself. Also, it's more important to relax and enjoy my work, rather than struggle for an ideal that is impossible to achieve.

Don't strive to be perfect; aspire only to create with love, enthusiasm and relish the journey in the process. Desiring constant perfection keeps one from accomplishing anything because it is impossible for us to attain. Demanding absolute flawlessness from ourselves at all costs is about ego, both in our work and in our lives. It's our ego telling us our work has to be better…better crafted, better received or better valued…than anyone else's. Whether there exists an underlying need to prove something to oneself or others, or simply craving the attention, ribbons or fame, the ego is certainly involved.

I am not saying you shouldn't try to achieve beautiful craftsmanship in your artwork. On the contrary, an exquisitely crafted work of art made with love is a joy to behold. However, when the goal is perfection, and it becomes an obsession, therein lies the problem. Perfectionism fueled by ego overshadows the joyous pilgrimage of creating. Amazingly, even when the perfectionist does produce extraordinary work, often the artist still perceives it as not quite good enough.

But a perfectionist isn't the only one to feel this way. Each of us is his or her own worst critic. Our eyes zero in on all the mistakes and should haves. To others our art looks wonderful. We need to learn to be patient with ourselves, especially the way we view and accept our own work.

Keep in mind it should not be your sole aim to produce a perfect quilt. Perfection is not the most important aspect of creating. It is, or should be, about the journey, your trek to artistic fulfillment. Rather than asking yourself, "Is my work flawless?" ask yourself these questions instead:

- Am I having fun with this project?
- Am I feeling satisfied and enjoying my creative journey?
- Am I growing both artistically and as a creative human being?
- How am I using my precious gift of creativity and for whose benefit?

Personal Notes

In my estimation, the last question is the most important. Creativity in any form is at its most glorious when we use it to help, inspire and serve others. As our creative abilities and talents are gifts from a Divine source, are we using these attributes for the betterment of others or for self-serving reasons? As an artist, which statement would you rather hear, "Your quilt is perfect" or "Your quilt touches my heart and comforts me?"

Consider the flowers and rocks in the fields, the fruits and vegetables we eat, all of the natural beautiful things we see around us. If you take a close look at each individual item, whether flower, rock, tree, fruit or whatever entity, you will notice few are perfect. Almost all have some type of flaw. That flaw doesn't diminish their beauty, meaningfulness or worthiness at all. In fact, that perfect looking piece of fruit doesn't taste any better than one with a mar and the perfect long-stemmed rose may not last as long or smell as sweet as the one with a short, curved stem and thorns you picked from your garden that morning.

It occurs to me that the Divine source, perfect and definitely capable of producing perfection, created all these objects that are not without blemish. So, why do we burden ourselves with the extra stress of being obsessive about the faults in our work? In fact, it is better to hope we are not so staunchly set on an ideal or our artistry will never blossom. We will have a difficult time finishing any of our projects because they will never measure up to our personal expectations. I read that artists in some cultures will intentionally include a mistake or flaw in their work. The gesture symbolizes humility and serves as a reminder to the artist that only God can achieve perfection.

Remember, with practice and repetition our technical expertise and creative artwork will develop and consistently improve with time, but it won't ever be flawless—and that is acceptable. Sometimes, those little mistakes and out-of-the-norm peculiarities make our quilt endearing to others, better defining our individual style and creating visual or emotional interest. If all art and life were perfect, life would be boring indeed.

Inevitably, as you finish each project, you will see something within it that displeases you and needs reworking. Change or fix whatever concept bothers you in your next

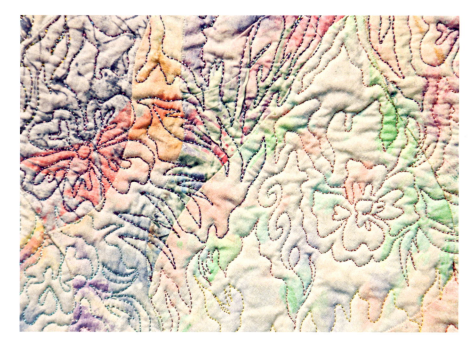

project. This restless desire for improvement is our creative spirit and mind struggling to achieve higher levels and goals. It is part of our growth as individuals and as artists.

On a personal note, in the past I struggled with perfectionism. Today, it continues to be a challenge, but not to the same extent it once was. I sometimes question the choices I make, fearful of making mistakes, not only in my art but also in everyday life. This type of thinking takes a toll. Now a bit wiser with age, I am able to catch myself more often when I fall into my perfection mode. I recognize the fear and anxiety involved with striving to obtain the unobtainable. As this is part of my makeup, all I can hope for is to acknowledge when the perfectionism kicks in and do my best to let it go and relax my attitude.

After the Storm (Detail, above): Flowers quilted in the sky.

After the Storm (Page 48): Seeking healing therapy through my art, I designed my first art quilt *Breaking Point*. *After the Storm*, a sequel, celebrates my husband's recovery from kidney cancer. The theme of *After the Storm* is one of inspiration and hope. Each of us faces personal storms and crises during our life, times when we feel the stormy winds and rains batter and beat us down. Strong roots of faith in God sustain us and we trust the storm will pass and the skies clear. After the storm, we hope for a life filled with happiness and serenity once more.

After the Storm (48˝ × 70˝)

Comparing the Two Quilts: I never make the same quilt design twice. However, I felt a strong urge to remake *Breaking Point*. Although I started with the same pattern used for *Breaking Point*, the new quilt evolved and turned out to be completely different. I made *After the Storm* four years after *Breaking Point*. By this time, we've weathered the storm of Denny's illness, and he is recovered and doing well. There are no signs of reoccurrence of his cancer. I am happier, more relaxed and less stressed.

Breaking Point

Compare these two quilts side by side. I did not intentionally plan the changes in *After the Storm*. My emotional state of mind during the construction of *After the Storm* was vastly different than when I created *Breaking Point*. This transformation is apparent in my design and color choices. Consider both trees. In *After the Storm*, the tree has grown larger, stronger and has three-dimensional texture. Its roots are longer and deeper. In *Breaking Point*, the sky is dark and ominous. In *After the Storm*, the storm has passed and is no longer a threat. The blue skies on the horizon promise happiness and peace. I quilted the clearing sky near the horizon with flowers to symbolize joy. There are more flowers on the ground, too. The overall emotional feeling of *Breaking Point* is one of chaos, anxiety and foreboding. In *After the Storm*, the menacing feeling is gone. The scene is more tranquil and relaxed.

These two quilts are wonderful examples showing when one works from the heart, from deep within one's core, the emotions inside flow into the artwork.

Courage

When I give a lecture, I attribute my lesson in courage to *After the Storm*. While making this quilt I started to experiment with different and unusual ways to broaden my basic curves and topstitch techniques.

I realized when one works exclusively on the top surface of a project, the possibilities for experimentation and creativity are endless. It is easier to implement all the color placement, piecing, construction, sewing, added dimension, texture, fabric manipulations and finishing techniques on the top surface, much more so than with conventional "right sides together" methods.

After the Storm was my first effort in working with texture and dimension. Once the quilt top was completed and sewn, but before it was sandwiched, I chose the patches I wanted to make dimensional. Usually they were the highlighted areas of the leaves and tree trunk. I marked each patch with a straight pin and flipped the quilt top over to the back. I was able to make small slits in the stabilizer foundation of the marked patches. Using needle-nose tweezers, I stuffed the area between the surface fabric and stabilizer with fiberfill, and then sealed the slit with fusible web. When all the patches were

stuffed and sealed, I layered the quilt top with the batting and backing fabric and quilted the sandwich. I quilted less heavily around the stuffed patches to enhance the dimensional height I wished to produce. The final result was a trapunto-style effect on the quilt's surface.

Thus, this project started a whole new dimension to my teaching as well as to my quilting. Once again, quilting taught me another lesson. Because I had the courage to experiment with *After the Storm*, I learned that courage, in all aspects of the word, is important in both quilting and life. Creative souls are not afraid to work with new ideas nor worry how

After the Storm (Opposite page): Detail of texture in the leaves. Many comment on the "duck" sitting on the tree branches. The duck was unintentional and did not appear until the surface was quilted.

Child's Play: Back art on *After the Storm*. This back art is a nostalgic look back to when I was younger and life was simpler. What I perceived as a difficulty or problem then is "child's play" compared to life's problems I encounter as I grow older.

others judge their art. They think and play freely without expectations, self-judgment or predetermined outcomes and express their thoughts about their work without fear. They have the courage to work intuitively and spontaneously. They do not create solely to please others, but to satisfy, explore, fulfill, indulge, heal, delight and nurture the artistic need within their mind, body and spirit.

For years, my daughter, Denise, has called me goody-two shoes. I suppose it's true. Through my entire life, even as a teen, I followed every one of the laws of life, society and of the nation to the letter. I've never had even so much as a parking ticket in all my years of driving. However, when it comes to creativity and my art, my dormant alter ego comes alive. Rebellion takes over. I have no qualms about breaking every rule in art with relish. In my mind, creativity has no rules. If you can think it, you can do it! Courage is the freedom to play and experiment with devilish abandon. Do you play it safe in your art? Do you have courage and let your imaginative alter ego loose?

Stretch, bend, break and shatter any rules that shackle your artistry and try new things. Courage is taking creative risks. In our world when you take a risk, ask yourself, "What are the best and worst outcomes?" You weigh the odds and then make a decision. In the creative world of quilting, the worst outcome I've experienced is that the idea I thought would work didn't pan out and I had to buy more fabric. This wasn't a problem for me, and probably won't be for any other fabric-addicted quilter either.

Allow yourself the freedom to consider all new avenues with avid curiosity. Do not strive for perfection or allow yourself to fear failure. There is no such thing as failure unless you give up and stop trying. Certainly, there will be setbacks and times when work will not go as planned. That is life. Setbacks are a necessary ingredient for creativity. You must experience adversities in order to grow.

Sadly, many talented quilters never attempt to design their own works because they are too timid. They play it safe. What they don't realize is that even if something goes wrong, it can be a proverbial silver lining and a tremendous opportunity for growth. Having a setback is an essential requirement for learning or we would not be forced to exercise our imaginations and seek creative solutions for problems. Without failure we remain complacent in our comfort zones and do not take inventive leaps of faith. From personal experience, I can tell you many of the artistic ideas in my quilts were born out of necessity, trying to hide or incorporate my unfortunate mistakes into workable solutions.

Curiosity

Innovative people are curious. They experiment. They discover. They dare to be different. Have a sense of adventure and try new things. Play and have fun. My two favorite mantras are "What if?" and "What do I have to lose?" These mantras should be yours as well.

Feed your curiosity. It is essential to your artistry. Be open to all things. Give yourself permission to have fun. Open all avenues and investigate different possibilities to enhance your work. Many times as you play, serendipity occurs.

Serendipity is discovering something good by happenstance. I call them happy accidents. For example, I love using multicolor, hand-dyed fabrics in my quilts. Due

to the dyeing processes, incidental splashes of other unplanned colors are contained in the fabric. The rogue colors are also present in every patch I cut out. The additional color splashes add depth and visual interest to the quilt. The quilt takes on a "painterly" look. As a former painter, I would have never thought of adding the daubs of color to my canvas in such a random manner. Using hand-dyed fabrics, the color splashes are serendipitous…happy accidents for me.

Before you begin a new project, do not concern yourself too much about analyzing and solving all the technical problems and details you may encounter.

Creation of the Sun and Stars (Detail): Chance colors in hand-dyed fabric add visual appeal and complexity to quilts.

If you expect to find the answers to all your questions and dilemmas before you start the project, chances are you will never begin. Overthink the problems and they will magnify in your mind. You will become overwhelmed and anxious. A scenario of seemingly insurmountable obstacles will haunt you.

In truth, there may be no way to know the answers to the problems until you actually experiment and work them out. Furthermore, you cannot know in advance exactly *what* problems you will face. Over the years and in every art form, I've always plunged headfirst into new projects without a safety net. Each time, I was able to work out solutions to the problems I encountered. I tackled each obstacle as it surfaced. The fixes became clear as the project progressed. Indeed, the resolutions and details were ones that I never could have imagined or foreseen in the design stages of the project. This brings to mind an old adage. "How do you climb a high mountain?" The answer is one step at a time.

I've learned if you keep an optimistic and relaxed mentality, the trials you experience in creating your artwork can be stepping-stones to new techniques, principles and designs. Errors are inevitable. The wisdom of searching for what can be learned from mishaps is invaluable and provides a wonderful opportunity for personal and artistic growth.

When exploring your curiosity, keep in mind art forms and concepts have no boundaries and may overlap. As quilters, consider using your photography, beading, weaving, crochet, felting, drawing, etc. to enrich your work. As artists, you have no limitations and may intermix favorite crafts. Try everything. You have nothing to lose, everything to gain.

Have Faith in Yourself

Once while giving a lecture and displaying my quilt, *Against All Odds*, a woman from the audience asked me, "I see you are using all types of different fabrics in your quilts. I use only cottons. How did you know to use fabrics other than cotton?" The question took me aback and it was a few

Creation of the Sun and Stars (Detail)

moments before I could answer her. I didn't think I had done anything out of the ordinary. My reply to her was, "Why *not* use other fabrics? It never occurs to me I can't use or do whatever is necessary to obtain the desired effect in my work." Later that evening, I thought more about her question and wondered why she would limit herself to using only cotton fabric in her work. One reason could be she simply had never been exposed to the idea of using other materials. But, I also think most of us fall prey to something else. We limit ourselves with barriers.

It is important to remember we have no restraints, either as artists or as the spiritual beings we are. It is our minds imposing all the restrictions. We tell ourselves what we can and cannot do, and then believe those limitations. As artists, we should be fearless and embrace creative opportunities. Don't confine or subject your artwork to conventional wisdom or rules of art if your inspiration tells you otherwise. March to your own inner wisdom, not the expectations of others or because that's the way it's always been done. Get to the point where you can joyfully say, "It never occurs to me I cannot do whatever I want in my artwork." Our dreams stop only with our imaginations.

Believe in your purpose and those dreams, even if others don't. Believe in yourself. Have faith in the work you do. Don't shy away from making a quilt or creating because you feel your efforts won't measure up to your or others' expectations. Never be intimidated by or compare yourself to other artists or their artwork. This advice is sometimes hard to follow. We tend to measure our work against others' and disparage or dismiss what we accomplish.

To have faith in yourself you must embrace a good attitude. Attitude is not only crucial, it is everything. Stay optimistic. A good can-do approach is essential for motivation and productive work. You'll never begin working on a quilt if you say to yourself, "I don't know how, so why start?" If you say, "I can't do it, so why bother?" you'll never finish the work. In turn, if you say, "I know I can do this," you will accomplish what you set out to do. Your mind does listen and believes what your voice tells it.

Remember all talents, creativity and inspirations emanate from a Divine source; these gifts are offered to each person on this earth. Although from one source, all talents aren't the same or distributed evenly. Though someone may possess more capability in a particular area or craft than you, your skills may well excel in another. What is most important is how we choose to use our special gifts.

Do not be influenced by another's advice regarding your work, no matter how well intentioned, if your innate feelings tell you otherwise. Trust your intuition and regard it as a tangible and essential part of your nature in life as well as art. Intuition is difficult to describe. It's a feeling of awareness, a small voice inside of us. One has to listen closely to hear this quiet murmur of inner wisdom. It is the guide keeping us on the right path and protecting us from peril. Yet many of us ignore or are hesitant to place trust in this silent whisper; we tend to second-guess our own instinctive feelings and instead heed the opinions of others.

For example, as a teacher, I see many students indecisive about which colors to use in class. Before giving my opinion, I always encourage the student to choose his or her own favorite among all the possible color choices. Almost every time the student will pick the color best suited for the quilt. The student's final response to me is, "That is the color I thought would work best, but I wanted to be sure."

The student instinctively knew from the beginning which color worked best, yet second-guessed his or her intuition, believing instead I must know more about color since I am the teacher. This is not true. I may have an opinion about what color I personally would use, but that doesn't make it the right choice for anyone else.

Making choices is subjective and personal. There is not just one way to do something correctly; there are *infinite* ways to do it correctly. We approach our art from different perspectives, experiences and places in our lives. What is a right choice for one is not necessarily right for all. A teacher cannot know what the student is trying to express, what message he or she is trying to communicate. Color choices make a huge difference in the overall mood of a quilt. Personal color selections made by the artist are what is important in a work, not those of an instructor.

The classroom exchange I just described between my student and me is a small example of what happens during almost every session I teach. Yet, I fear this simple lack of trust in one's own judgment can extend into other important areas of our lives as well. When will we learn to trust our own intuition?

In my personal experience, listening to my inner voice has never led me astray. That is not to say negative thoughts and fears do not sneak around the corners of my mind. They do, bringing doubt and fear with them. I constantly have to remind myself to have faith. Trusting my intuition has become easier with practice and mindfulness. I've become more confident in all my choices, whether life or art. Learn to listen to *your* inner voice and be confident. It will take practice, but the results will be worthwhile.

Confidence in your choices will help eliminate the greatest enemies of creativity, which are fear and procrastination. Many talented people don't trust their abilities or embark on a new project because of fear, anxious their work won't measure up to someone else's. They worry they lack the capability of doing the job perfectly. Tell me, why do you care what others think if the work represents your passion? Why compare your work to another's?

What is important is your work comes into being, not that it becomes a masterpiece hanging in a museum for all the world to behold. A work that springs from your mind and heart and made with loving hands has much value and worth. It tells a story of **you**. An expression of who you are and how you behold the world, your creation is important regardless of what price tag someone may attach to it.

Creation of the Sun and Stars (65ʺ × 75ʺ): The Creator's omnipresent power, represented by the yellow ribbons, flows from all corners of the heavens to form our sun, the cranberry orb. The newly born, spinning sun throws fire and flames back into the universe and eventually the flames transform into dancing stars. This quilt is a symbol of joy.

The Story Behind the Creation of the Sun and Stars

I love this quilt. Of all the quilts I've made to date, it is hands down my favorite and I consider it my masterpiece. I've often felt the inspiration for it was a special gift to me. *Creation of the Sun and Stars* is also the quilt that reinforced my faith in my work and myself.

The idea for this quilt came at 5:30 AM on a winter morning. It was my husband's day off from work and I was looking forward to sleeping in between nice, warm, toasty sheets. Of course, you know inspiration has no concept of time or convenience and so it was with this one. I didn't want to get out of my cozy bed. I nestled a little deeper under the covers, but the vision I saw in my mind for this quilt was amazing and I knew I had to sketch it before the image faded.

I always keep paper and a pencil in my nightstand drawer. Some of my best ideas come just before sleep or awaking in the morning when I'm relaxed. Still snug in my bed, I started to sketch the idea and make notes of what I envisioned, but quickly became engrossed in the drawing and went downstairs to work in earnest. Unbelievably, in very short order, within three hours or so, I had the whole design drawn out.

I started on my new quilt later that day. This large quilt was one of the quickest and easiest I've ever made. Everything flowed smoothly with no setbacks or problems. *Creation of the Sun and Stars* was, and still is, my pride and joy. And it *is* all about joy. I submitted *Creation of the Sun and Stars* to a major competition and it was accepted and sent off.

Months earlier I had the good fortune to meet two women, Susan Towner-Larsen and Barbara Brewer Davis, who were in the process of writing a book titled, *With Sacred Threads: Quilting and the Spiritual Life*. Their book's theme was about the correlation between spirituality and quilting. My quilt, The *Fire Within*, was included in the book's chapter on creativity. These authors also facilitated an inter-denominational retreat limited to sixteen women. As with the book, the focus of the retreat was the spirituality/quilting link.

This restful retreat, held at a lodge nestled in the woods, was a beautiful, uplifting experience. A wonderful spiritual energy and camaraderie flowed among us and we nourished one another. Strangers at the beginning of the retreat, we became kindred spirits at the end.

Students and teachers alike left the retreat three days later on an adrenaline high. During the drive home, the adrenalin faded and exhaustion set in. I couldn't wait to hit the couch for a little nap until my husband returned from work. When I walked through the front door, there was a box lying on the floor containing my *Creation of the Sun and Stars*, finally home from the quilt show.

I opened the box to make sure "my baby" was OK. On top of the tissue wrappings was a folder with the show booklet and the lone judge's review. I couldn't resist. As I started to read the statement, the smile on my face turned to disbelief. The quilt had minus marks for innovation and color. The statement said, "You should add touches to make it your own" and "There is only so much you can do with a spiral."

My first thought was, "Could they have mixed up my judge's review with another entrant's quilt?" I had faith in this quilt and knew deep down it was a worthy piece. As a veteran of quilt shows, I also knew whether a quilt places in a competition is subjective and has no bearing on the meaningfulness or value of one's work. Nor do judges' opinions reflect one's merit as an artist.

Nonetheless, the review bothered me and I wasn't able to take that nap I so desperately needed. As I lay there, I thought about the reasons it might have warranted such a scathing review. At one point, I wondered if it might have anything to do with the mention of the "Creator" in the artist's statement and the spiritual implication of the quilt's theme.

What popped into my mind next was, "There is no safe haven for these types of quilts dealing with personal issues or spirituality." The very next thought, an unwelcome inspiration, was, "You have to start one." At once, the details for a new show started to pour from my mind. I should name it "Sacred Threads" and convene the exhibition every two years. The categories would be joy, spirituality, inspiration, healing and grief. The exhibit should include an array of interdenominational quilts, celebrating the spirituality that transcends organized religion. Unlike other shows, the focus should be on the feelings and emotional aspects of the artists' work, not centered solely on art or workmanship that is the traditional basis for current exhibitions. The quilts were not to be judged, as there is no way to judge one's emotions. And no age restrictions imposed on the quilts accepted for the show, as the stories and symbolism they depict are timeless and relevant regardless of when the pieces were made. The names of the persons I should ask for help, Barbara, Susan and my students from the retreat, were forefront in my mind.

I did not take this barrage well at all. In fact, I was unnerved and distressed by the unwanted and eerie notions that came to mind. And they would not stop. I fought back hard. For every detail that materialized, I had a good reason why I couldn't say yes to this idea of *Sacred Threads*. I had no expertise or experience with organizing anything, let alone a quilt show. Nor did I have the money it would require to do it. Still, the idea persisted.

I decided to phone the women whose names came into my mind. I reasoned once they said no, I could relax and take my nap. So one by one, I called everyone on my list. To my dismay, each one of them thought it was a fantastic idea and said yes except one…Wendy Bynner. "Finally, someone with sense," I thought to myself. Forty minutes later Wendy called me back. "I don't know what it is," she told me. "I can't say no to this." I knew why.

Thus, we began organizing *Sacred Threads* for a target date of July 2001. I was anxious and worried, but somehow everything fell together beautifully and the money appeared, seemingly from nowhere. A stroke of luck? No. This show had a definite purpose.

Sacred Threads 2001 was a hit and touched so many people, the artists as well as the viewers. At the end of the show, we still had enough money to start planning for the next show in 2003.

Unbelievably organized, tireless and indispensable, Wendy was vital for *Sacred Threads*' existence. She became my co-chair, then chairwoman, until we both retired after curating the 2009 show. *Sacred Threads* lives on through another committee member, Lisa Ellis, and the exhibition has found a new home in Washington, D.C. where it will continue to move peoples' spirits and touch their hearts for many years to come.

This is the true story of how one judge's opinion and my faith in *Creation of the Sun and Stars* started a national quilt exhibition. It occurred to me several years later had the review been any less upsetting, I would have ignored it and thrown the evaluation in the wastebasket. That would have been the alternate ending to this story. The review had to be as it was or *Sacred Threads* wouldn't exist.

Through it all, I learned something else as well. At one point, I remember visualizing myself standing outside an open window, looking in, detaching myself from the situation I guess. I could see clearly how everything was falling into place for *Sacred Threads*, almost as if by magic. It was flowing smoothly without any major glitches along the way. I remember the amazement when I first realized what was happening before my eyes. It was then I understood. This show was meant to be and it was out of my hands. I was not the one in control, only the facilitator. With this insight, I began to relax and not worry. What needed to happen for this show to exist would transpire. I learned how one's attitude toward life *should* flow.

To this day, I try to maintain that same accepting way of thinking about everything in my life. It's not easy; I was born a worrywart. With my new outlook, everyday disappointments in life seldom affect me anymore. I know everything works out in my best interest, even though it doesn't appear to be true at the time.

For example, in the past when a wonderful teaching opportunity fell through for me, I would be extremely upset and disappointed. Today when the same situation arises, I am not the least bothered. I know when the timing is right for all involved, I will teach when and where I'm needed.

These days when a touchy circumstance arises, I stand outside that window watching for the flow and knowing it will all work out as it should. I'm the first to admit I don't have my "no worry" technique perfected yet, but I'll keep trying.

Passion

Passion is the most important emotion of a creative person. It is an intense fire burning within you. You are ablaze with ardor and excitement. You are eager and committed. Passion is a strong force of dedication and enthusiasm for the work you do. Moreover, enthusiasm breeds creativity. Passion is love of life.

Inspired artists put their feelings, sentiments, love and zeal into their work as well as in other facets of their lives. A genuine and original artistic style evolves from reaching deep within your core and allowing fervor and enthusiasm to flow through your hands and into your quilt. Through my creative journey, I learned to produce art that satisfies the thirst within my soul, heals my body and feeds my spirit. I do not create only to please others.

The Fire Within: Our Spirit of Creativity (64˝ × 62 ½˝)**:** I felt I was not alone when I created *The Fire Within*. My hands could not work fast enough. I was able to create with total concentration and focus, almost trance-like. Once I'd stop working, there were times I couldn't remember constructing various elements. It was not only me creating. There was someone working with me, guiding me.

The Fire Within became a spiritual encounter for me. A host of adjectives describing this experience comes to mind, among them fearful awe, elation, eerie and unnerving. I would take many solitary walks to center myself and shed many tears, but not from unhappiness or joy. The tears were a release from a feeling of being completely overwhelmed; I would explode if I tried to hold them in.

I still experience feelings such as this now and again when I create, but never to the extent as I did for *Fire Within*. It is truly a special quilt. Made and dedicated in thanksgiving to the Holy Spirit for a talent I didn't realize I possessed until I reached my forties, The *Fire Within* embodies my passion and joyfulness.

For the artist, allowing intense emotions to spring forth freely in one's work restores the spirit and the calms the mind. This release provides the artist with a gratifying sense of relief, liberation, cleansing and achievement.

Fire Within: Our Spirit of Creativity (Detail)

Artwork mirrors one's essence and reflects whom that person is deep within. It's a canvas emanating from the soul revealing how one deals personally with life's situations and changes.

Art created with passion is extraordinary because it conveys unspoken emotions and thoughts to all who see the work. It is easily apparent and the viewer of the artwork will readily recognize the mindset of the maker. If one creates without heart and spirit, the viewer will see that as well.

One can feel deeply about issues and situations, good, bad and controversial and include those opinions in his or her work. Many times quilts made with moving statements on sensitive or uncomfortable issues, such as spirituality, disease, abuse or grief will come across as disquieting to the viewer. These works, although they cause uneasiness in our comfort zones, make us aware of the problems and issues that face us in today's world. Some people may find comfort from quilts depicting unsettling issues and others may be upset. When one views quilts on display in exhibitions such as *Sacred Threads*, a show emphasizing emotional perspectives and focusing on passionate issues, it becomes evident the artist has power to touch hearts and affect others in ways beyond imagination.

In *Sacred Threads* each participating exhibitor is requested to write an artist's statement. Usually, an artist's statement includes a description of the materials used and explains how the quilt was constructed. For *Sacred Threads* the participant must explain *why* he or she made the quilt, the reason for the quilt's existence. This statement is just as important as the piece itself for the show's purpose. As a result, the narratives submitted by the artists often give personal, emotional insights into their spirits.

In the past, we supplied comment sheets for viewers. We encouraged them to write notes to the artists regarding their piece, particularly if a quilt was a favorite or spoke to them. Most wrote a sentence or a paragraph, but many wrote an entire letter to the artist. We included these notes when we shipped the quilts home at the end of the exhibit.

Besides the juried entries from artists, we also included a themed special exhibit in each biennial show. The special exhibit that towered above all others was *Beyond the Barrier* from our 2009 Exhibition. Most of the women who created the seventeen quilts in this special exhibit were not quilters or sewers. Nor would our society consider them artists. They were inmates in a central Ohio women's prison.

How *Beyond the Barrier* came to be included in *Sacred Threads 2009* is a story itself. Not too long after our exhibit in the summer of 2007, I attended a church service. The gospel included passages about "feeding the hungry, taking care of the ill and visiting those in prison." I can remember thinking, "I don't know anyone in prison. Whom would I visit? How could this passage possibly pertain to me?"

Have you ever heard of the word, "synchronicity?" Synchronicity is defined as one or more chance happenings, coincidences that seemingly have no direct connection, yet they are physically, mentally or spiritually significant to the person involved. Synchronicity seems to happen to me often. Maybe it's only because I sense when it does occur. What happened after the church service is perhaps one of my best examples of synchronicity.

Not more than a few days after asking myself how this gospel passage could pertain to me, I received an email from the chaplain at the women's reformatory. She explained she had attended our 2007 exhibition and was deeply touched by the quilts. She asked if I would speak and present a slide show about the exhibition for some of the inmates. In particular, she requested I include thirty quilts from the healing and grief categories. She said these thirty quilts would be especially meaningful to the women. When I read her email, I was stunned. My mind flew back to my thoughts and questions from the church service a few days earlier. The goose bumps spread all over my body. I knew this email was not a coincidence.

Wendy Bynner, my *Sacred Threads* co-chairwoman; my husband, Denny; my sister, Augustine and I went to the prison for the presentation. Both Wendy and I spoke about the exhibit, showed slides and read the artists' statements. The women were visibly moved, with many in tears. The whole experience was amazing and eye-opening. The spirituality flowing in the room was palpable.

The chaplain inquired if the inmates could submit quilts into our 2009 show. Although most of the women had never made a quilt, they were excited about the idea of putting their own stories and thoughts into cloth. Of course, we agreed but said they would have to submit to the same jury process as the other entrants. They had about a year and a half to complete their work. When the chaplain dropped off the quilts for our jury consideration, it was obvious to us that we needed to display all seventeen. We knew we had our special exhibit for 2009.

The women who submitted these quilts did not have sewing machines. They did all their sewing by hand. The only fabrics they had to work with were the varying types of material donated to them. For most of the women, the completed work was their first quilt. While most of the seventeen quilts would be considered too primitive by current fiber art or quilt show standards, these works turned out to be the highlight of our 2009 show.

These women, inexperienced in art and quilting, and using only donated materials, worked from their hearts and souls. Despite their limitations, the quilts they made told powerful, heartfelt stories. The women depicted their spiritual beliefs, their journeys, their dreams and family circumstances. Viewers stood riveted as they read the artists' statements and studied the quilts. Even though separated by prison bars, these inmates had the power to touch and communicate, intensely affecting others through their simple, but poignant, works of art.

During our exhibitions, I discovered much from observing people's reactions to the quilts and by reading and listening to their comments. I cannot count the number of people who approached me during and after the shows, all expressing excitement, passionate feelings and encouraging sentiments about *Sacred Threads*. The valuable lessons I learned are ones no school can teach and is knowledge I'll never forget and always try to communicate to my students.

What are the lessons learned? I discovered art created with passion has more impact on viewers. When we share ourselves through our work, others connect with us. We are all human and at one time or another, we walk the same path of life's experiences, both joyful and sorrowful. Art created with passion is a profoundly meaningful, non-verbal communication with others and strongly touches emotions. Passionate work moves hearts and souls and radiates energy. People contemplate emotion-filled work. They study the piece with focused attention, engrossed in its message. They remember. Art touches a chord deep within and can be cathartic. People connect with the topic and relate it to their own joys, beliefs, crises or sorrows. They laugh. They cry. They rejoice. They heal.

Passion's effects do not stop with the viewers. It is beneficial to the artist as well. Do you remember the comment sheets from the exhibitions? We received wonderful feedback from many artists. They were thrilled with the notes, letters and remarks they received. The artists expressed appreciation and gratitude, knowing their work was a comfort or had touched the heart and spirit of another. They told us the comments from the viewers were rewarding to them and the comments justified and validated their work. Thus, the communication between the artists and viewers provided value for both.

Have you discovered the fire within? What is your passion, your fire? Are you aflame with enthusiasm for the work you do? Do you consistently put passion into your artwork? Your life?

Personal Notes

Never be afraid to immerse your heart and soul into your art. Enjoy what you do and do it enthusiastically. Now, muster your courage. Put your passionate feelings into a new quilt.

Ability to Share Your Work and Yourself

Resting Place (Detail)

Once you include your innermost thoughts and emotions in your art, I hope you'll find the strength and courage to share it with others. From my childhood years until now, I've always followed the religious tenets of my upbringing, but anxiously struggling with Denny through his bout with cancer boosted my faith even more. During that time, the adversity in our lives awakened a dormant spirituality and heightened insight within me.

Of all the art forms I've used over the years, my healing quilt, *Breaking Point*, was the first piece to embrace symbolism. From then on, I increasingly included symbolism or spiritual and moral philosophies in my quilts. However, including spirituality in my art was neither planned nor deliberate; it wasn't until years later I realized the effect it had on my work. Intuitively, I was releasing my deepened faith and hope into my art, as well as my stresses and anxiety.

As I've said so many times, when you work from your heart and deep within your soul, what is inherent within you surfaces in your art. As my spirituality intensified after that tumultuous time in my family's lives, so did the spirituality included within my art. At first, I was concerned about exposing my thoughts and feelings, fearing others might misunderstand my motives or criticize. Then it occurred to me my work was no different in symbolism or spirituality than the exquisite stained glass windows that I loved as a teen or the religious-based paintings hanging in art museums today.

Sometimes we worry about what others think of us. We don't want to show our frailties or open ourselves up to rebuke. Yes, creating is therapeutic to the mind and spirit and it is fulfilling to be sure. But, when you share it with others, you open

yourself to the possibility of misinterpretation and judgment. If you allow it to, this criticism can destroy a fragile self-esteem.

For instance, early in my teaching career I shared my newly constructed quilt, *Portrait of My Soul* (page 41), with someone whom I considered a peer. Though I did not want or ask for critique, to my amazement this person began to severely cut down the artistry and ridiculed the quilt to the point I was rendered speechless. Stunned to think my new piece was worthless as art, I sought the guidance of a friend, a fine arts professor at a local university. As I repeated what my quilting colleague said, the professor just shook her head. "There is not a thing wrong with this quilt", she assured me. I told her after hearing such scathing remarks I was uncomfortable showing it to anyone else or submitting it into competition. The professor replied, "You will enter this quilt and you will be proud of it." I persisted and asked her if there was any positive critique she could offer. She told me, "The only thing I can possibly advise is when you draft your design, make sure you vary the size, space and mass of all the templates. You don't want them to be the same or similar size. There is more visual interest if the sizes of the patches differ." I asked her how I could thank her for the encouragement. She told me to pass on the advice to my students. To this very day, I include her valuable design information in every class I teach.

As it turned out, my friend was right. I did submit this quilt into national competitions and it won many ribbons, including two first places finishes… one at the largest quilt show in the United States. This incident taught me yet another valuable lesson about the importance of having faith in your inspirations, yourself and sharing your work with others. There could have been an alternate outcome. It would have been

Resting Place (66½" × 87"): This quilt depicts the vastness and serenity of the Rocky Mountains. During a family hike, we stopped to rest at a beautiful site on the trail. Enamored with my surroundings, I was reluctant to leave. Even though many years have passed, I still feel as if part of my spirit, depicted by the ribbon transparency, lovingly remains there. My spirit is joyful and in total harmony with the mountains, water and earth.

Both quilts, *Resting Place* and *Portrait of My Soul* (page 41) enable me to share my spirit with others.

easy to dwell on my peer's spiteful words. Easy to take them to heart, say nothing and let the hurt fester inside my mind. This course might have affected my future work or possibly even my decision to continue quilting. Rather, I had to remind myself criticism is only another's opinion; that is all it is, an opinion.

As humans we seek justification and acceptance, so when someone praises our work we are happy and proud, but upset when one disapproves. Whether rave review or pan, both are only evaluations, judgments that are subjective to the attitudes, thoughts, life experiences and issues of the reviewer. This holds true whether it is a single critical review or from many. Opinions do not dictate the worth of our work or us. Follow your heart. You are entitled to the creative choices you make. Always stand by your work no matter how others accept it.

In my quilting career I've had my share of criticism. More often than not, I discovered these moments were disguised opportunities and in each instance good resulted from the situation. You cannot be hurt from criticism unless you allow it to harm you. Overwhelmingly, I've found the rewards I've reaped from sharing my work far outweigh the bad comments. To be able to touch a heart or stir another's soul with your artwork is priceless. In my mind, it is the most cherished treasure of all.

It is my personal philosophy we are instruments of God. We must have faith in our abilities to be conduits, to use our art to communicate, reach out and connect with others. Remember, we share a common thread of problems. Opening up by sharing our difficulties with others who are sympathetic and sincere can lead to solutions and healing for our personal issues as well as theirs.

After more than seventeen years of teaching and lecturing, it still astonishes me I can speak to audiences that often number in the hundreds. During my school years, I seldom raised my hand in class due to shyness and fear of making mistakes in front of classmates. Now, without fear or anxiety, I openly tell my listeners the stories behind my quilts. I also discuss my personal experiences, my blunders and the wisdom learned from them.

Before every lecture, I always review my notes to refresh my memory. I also pray the words I speak will be meaningful and those who need to hear them will be able to connect with those words. After almost every lecture, people will approach me to say how much my presentation affected and pertained to them on a personal level. Uncannily, they will repeat, almost verbatim, words I prayed before the lecture. When these occurrences first happened, I was shocked and unnerved. I felt as if someone wanted me to know my prayers were acknowledged. But these days, rather than being startled, I calmly chalk it up to the synchronicity I now recognize in my life. At this point, I know on my deepest level I am where I should be and doing what I am supposed to do at any particular moment. Though filled with doubt at the beginning of my teaching career, I've learned to trust my students will be able to learn from my art and experiences.

You should learn to trust as well. Expect the people who will benefit most from your work will be guided to it, and your work will speak to them. Have faith people will interpret your art in ways that are most helpful to them. I'm always amazed when people tell me how much they are drawn to one of my quilts. They may find healing, comfort or joy in the quilt as it touches them on a very personal level. They relate, but on their own terms, reading into the quilt what they need to see depending on what is going on in their lives at the moment. Often, the message they hear and profit from is not the message I intended to convey when I created the quilt. You cannot know or guess, nor understand why or how, your creation will impact another. I believe God works through us, using our creative abilities to communicate with and help others, with or without our knowledge.

As a teacher I've always freely revealed anything about myself, my secrets for construction techniques and inspirations without hesitation. I've always felt inspiration is intended to flow through us to encourage and communicate to others. Unbelievably, I've found the more I give away, the more creative inspiration I receive. It just keeps coming.

Do not hesitate to offer your creativity and insights to others. We possess many gifts, talents and abilities; they are intended to be shared. Give away these spiritual gifts generously. As they come from an abundant source, they will be replenished.

My sister, Augustine, once gave me this advice: Pass on to others what you have learned, share knowledge, and in return, learn what others have to teach you. In our earthly lives, there must be equal give and take to be in balance. If we find ourselves at either end of the spectrum, all giving or all taking, we lose our sense of equilibrium and interconnection between others and ourselves. We may lose the respect of others as well. We cannot always take. We must learn to give our knowledge freely to others.

Equally important, be open and willing to receive insight from friends, family, artists and strangers alike. Acknowledge them. Realize they have something of value to offer. Welcome their knowledge and priceless gift of wisdom. Accepting these offerings bestows energy, respect and joy to both parties.

Motivation

We live in a hectic world. Getting caught up in the busy day's schedule makes it difficult to stay motivated and focused on quilting. We feel as if we are stretching in a dozen different directions, yet our energy and time are limited. Our work, family needs, friends and the demands of everyday life get in the way, making it a challenge to concentrate or stay focused on the art of quiltmaking.

We are battered from constant distractions like the phone, TV and computers that are part of the daily routine. Many of us are addicted to cell phones and email. Noise surrounds us all day, both the sounds we actually hear and the constant, inner thoughts buzzing through our minds. We can turn off outside

Pond Reflections at Dawn (Detail)

We can use determination to keep the distractions at bay and help us stay on track. Prioritize your quilting goals. How important is quilting in your life at this moment? Is it a comfort or healing therapy for you? A hobby? A career? Are physical limitations or temporary emotional setbacks a problem for you right now?

sources of noise, but the clamor of our minds can be difficult if not impossible to still, especially if we are anxious, stressed or upset. These distractions hinder our artistic productivity. Stop now and give some thought to this question. What stops *you* from being productive?

Personal Notes

Pond Reflections at Dawn (61" × 76½" × 76½"): This triangular quilt is an improvisational, abstract scene from Blacklick Pond. It is my interpretation of curvy log cabin blocks.

Realistically, look at how much time you can allot to your quilting or other artwork. Consider the best ways to cut down on diversions during your day such as turning off the computer, TV and cell phone.

Don't let daily disruptions waste your precious resources. If you cannot devote blocks of your day to your quilting, then work in small increments whenever you can break away. It's advantageous to intentionally set aside a moment or an hour to work on your project. Reserve as much time as you can for your art and creatively exploring new ideas. Once you decide on duration, whether daily or weekly, make written notations on your calendar for the specific periods you'll allocate to your projects. The simple act of writing down a commitment in your schedule will give your action energy and validity. Hold yourself to working during these reserved times whether you feel creative or not. By faithfully adhering to your plan you'll develop the *habit* of working on your art.

The secret to being productive is consistency. Getting into the habit of working a few minutes a day, every day, will add up to a finished quilt. Your determination will make a difference here. Resolve to find the time to quilt and you *will* discover a way to do it.

Many times the hardest part of any task is physically getting started in the first place. If you are having difficulty becoming motivated, the simple act of initiating work on a project may help you get a second wind. Take out some fabric and notions and begin to work. Chances are motivation will kick in and take over.

I used this premise one New Year's Day when my husband was watching a boring football game, at least it was to me. Restless and at loose ends, I didn't feel like working on my art either. Nonetheless, I talked myself into going to my studio. Once there, motivation kicked in. I decided to try something new with scraps of expensive fabric and miscellaneous patches left over from previous quilts. After exploring the possibilities, I created an improvisational quilt titled *Pond Reflections at Dawn*. This experience was a major breakthrough for me; it marked the beginning of including improvisational techniques in my artwork and classroom teachings.

If motivation is a problem for you, make a conscious effort to determine the underlying reasons. What are you feeling at the time? Many times, once we recognize and acknowledge the problem while it is happening, we can overcome or diffuse the situation and become productive.

I admit that getting motivated is a challenge for me. I am not as productive as I wish I could, or think I should be. As a busy teacher constantly on the road, I tell myself I'm too tired physically and mentally to work on a project. And to an extent that's true. But it goes deeper than that.

From personal experience I've noticed, like other rhythms in my body, the strength of my creativity ebbs and flows. Sometimes my creativity is strong and active and I am productive. Other times it is upsettingly quiet. I wonder if I've lost my edge.

Realize you cannot turn creativity on and off at any given moment. It doesn't work that way. I'm sure from past experience you've noticed you must be in the mood to work well and with vision. When moving from teaching to creative mode, it can take anywhere from a week to two months or more for me to switch gears. Once I am in my quilting mode, I thrive on challenge. But if I'm not feeling inspired or enthusiastic, I find myself procrastinating and coming up with every excuse not to work. Take a look at the following list. Notice most of the reasons are based on emotional and mental feelings rather than physical causes.

I searched within to discover the underlying reasons hindering my motivation, whether related to art or not. I compiled a list of the most common:

- I have no desire to do the project or business at hand. It is something I have to do, not *want* to do. I have no passion for the project and find every excuse to put it off.
- I am completely overwhelmed. There is so much busyness in my life, I can't think straight or prioritize my tasks. I shut down and do nothing.
- I am unsure or don't know what to do (write, design, create, name your own verb) next in the situation at hand. My mind is blank and I am at a loss. I can't come to a decision. I putter around the house or do something else instead.

- I lose focus or excitement for the work.
- I feel frustration, fear or anxiety. What if what I am doing doesn't measure up or is not well-received?
- My spiritual well is empty, drained. I've given it all away. I feel exhausted and as though there is nothing left within me.

The most common ways I procrastinate from my work are:

- Snack on something unhealthy and eat chocolate (comfort food).
- Take unnecessary, frequent and extended breaks when I should be working.
- Find something else I would rather do or work on, usually unimportant.
- Make excuses and allow myself to become distracted by non-priority activities such as getting involved with the breaking news of the day on TV, unnecessary phone calls, errands, constantly checking email, researching something unrelated on the internet and other such actions.
- Play just a few games of free-cell solitaire on the computer. For me, "just a few" games can turn into hours of non-productive activity. I like to blame this addiction on my husband. He taught me how to play.

Do these excuses sound familiar? Often I engage in stalling techniques without thinking. Once I pay attention to what I am doing, it is easier for me to regroup and get back on track. Being cognizant of what I am doing and why I do it has been a tremendous help for me to stay motivated. What is keeping you from moving forward on your project? What are your favorite procrastination activities? Try to become conscious of your actions and jot down your notes in a journal. My guess is once you become fully aware of what impedes your creativity, your motivation will improve as well.

Personal Notes

On the flip side, I think it is helpful to determine what encourages one to be motivated. What fuels your motivation? For me, it is:

- Passion. The work is something I want to do and feel strongly about. Learn to say no whenever possible to things in your life that do not spark the passion in you.
- Excitement. I am full of enthusiasm for the project. Just thinking about trying new techniques, approaches, mediums or materials energizes me.
- I get an incredible vision, inspiration or a new idea for a particular new quilt or design.
- Staying spiritually centered. I do my best when I feel blessed and my soul nourished.
- Interacting, working with and being inspired by other kindred spirits. For me, the energy and mutual support of being with other artists is stimulating and motivational.

Interacting with others is a major source of motivation. It is a wonderful yin/yang of give and take. Creativity begets even more creativity. I am energized and motivated by my students' imaginations and inventiveness when I teach. Their energy plays off every person in the room. It is abundant and tangible. The excitement flowing from my students is simply amazing, and I am forever grateful and inspired by them. I may teach and lead my class but, in return, my students offer me the joys of motivation, inspiration and knowledge.

Rhapsody in Pink (Detail)

Creativity

The generic dictionary definition of creativity is the capability to develop original and imaginative thought. My personal definition of creativity in art is utilizing individual thoughts, points of view and life experiences to interpret an idea or design so that it becomes one's own. The way an individual sees and interprets an idea, color, design, or an object such as a flower, tree or the ocean can be opposite from another's perspective. Each of us is unique with our own quirks and idiosyncrasies. We react to our surroundings in a different way. If one hundred people created a quilt using the same live tree as a subject, each would vary from the other ninety-nine. This is a valuable opportunity for us. This diverse interpretation of nature or life in our artwork makes it distinctive and visually interesting to others. Speaking personally, I'd rather see how an artist conveys an image in a quilt, a flower perhaps, using her or his perspective and self-expression rather than realism. One can see realism in a snapshot. Visually, a flower conceived through another's eyes, spirit and imagination is far more exciting and captivating than a flower perfectly reproduced from a photograph. Self-expression is a far more satisfying experience for the artist as well.

It is diverse beliefs, viewpoints and personal life events that give art individuality. When we find the courage to combine all these concepts, strive to express them freely and incorporate them in our work, we acquire a creative touch we can call our own authentic style and approach to art. We put ourselves, what we are, our entire being, into our art. You can copy another's design or look, but if you want to develop your own distinctive style, you must portray your subject matter using your individual slant, perspective and interpretation. Your artistic style is unique and yours alone.

By incorporating favorite techniques, colors, lines, objects, etc. in quilting we develop our own originality and characteristics that become easily recognizable to others and set us apart as imaginative. As with our bodies, imagination and creativity become stronger the more we exercise them. Ultimately, the definition of creativity is the ability to immerse our hearts, minds and spirits into interpreting ideas or designs in our art.

I believe the uniqueness each one of us possesses is a special gift from a higher being. We should strive to take advantage of our diversity and incorporate these individual perspectives into our art. Recognize that our personal thoughts are interesting to others and they can be meaningful to people who view our work.

Each of us is a creative person, but in many different ways. Talents and abilities, gifts from the Divine, vary widely from one person to another. The ways we use our gifts and to what extent also differ. Many times I will hear from one of my students, "I'm not a creative person." That is simply not true. Perhaps this person's talent in visual art is not on a level that allows her or his work to hang in a museum with world acclaim. Talents, and the passion to use them, are not equal in all persons. But the creative gifts and abilities the individual possesses in other areas may far surpass those of the artist whose work is hanging in the museum.

Everyday life is creative: gardening, writing, cooking, journaling, throwing a party, helping others, caregiving. Even routine housework or decision-making can be inspired ventures. The list is endless. You probably do not realize how resourceful you really are. You may not consider what you do during your busy day as imaginative, but it is. You are creative all day long but do not acknowledge it.

From this point forward, choose to think about everything you do from a different perspective. Rather than seeing the daily actions you perform as simple, mundane tasks, instead focus on the skill, inventiveness and energy you need to perform these activities. In short, be conscientiously aware of your creativity. Awareness gives you energy. Be mindful of when and how you are creative. No matter how seemingly unimportant or small the task at hand, recognizing your creativity allows you to appreciate, be grateful for and cherish your wonderful abilities and talents.

Honor your creativity. Nurture and feed it with energy. Afford it the power of movement and momentum. One idea will flow into another, then another. So take time now to make a list of your creative endeavors from the past few days on these pages or in your journal. Be attentive and be grateful.

Creativity

Personal Notes

Rocky Mountain Wildflowers (36˝ × 39˝): *Rocky Mountain Wildflowers* is my tribute to the beautiful alpine meadows in the Rocky Mountain National Park in Colorado. All the flowers and most leaves are three-dimensional and project from the quilt's top surface. The fuzzy moss in the detail (inset) was constructed by machine felting wool fibers and dyed cheesecloth on a foundation of water-soluble stabilizer. The moss collage was attached to the surface with free-motion stitching.

Creativity

I consider creativity as spiritual practice and a personal form of devotion. Being an imaginative person is imitating the Creator whether we realize it or not. Because the Creator is involved with our inspirations and is limitless in ideas, the possibilities for quilts,

art, music and other dreams are endless. The impossible is possible. God uses each of us as an intermediary. Through our actions, words, gifts and talents, we are able to touch, heal and guide others.

We need to search for, recognize, appreciate and utilize the talents we've been given. How many times when inspirations and ideas come to us do we say, "No." or "Maybe later when I have more energy and time." or "After the kids are grown and I retire?" It takes trust and sometimes a scary leap of faith to say yes and act on our inspirations.

Rhapsody in Pink (Detail; full size is 36˝ × 32˝): Water lilies and lily pads floating in a pond are one of my favorite things to see in nature. I imagine them to be alive and dancing for joy, swaying to the music of the gentle breeze in the presence of the Creator.

Make it a habit to acknowledge inspirations when you are blessed to experience them. They are gifts offered to us. If we don't take action, they will be given to another who is receptive and interested in accepting the challenge. Have you ever experienced the following scenario: You get a wonderful inspiration for a new quilt, but you delay beginning it for whatever reason. Lo and behold, a short time later, another person comes up with the identical idea and actually creates your quilt. I think the timing of the inspiration is significant. The quilt's purpose or message needs to be out in the world. If we ignore the call, inspiration goes elsewhere.

Staying spiritually centered encourages the creative process. Additionally, resist any negative thought and instead be optimistic in attitude. From a personal perspective, I find when I expect the best I get it. And when I expect less, I get that too. Realize and concentrate on your abundance of gifts and talents, not what you perceive to be missing in your life.

Search intently for serenity within. Practice the sacred art of listening for the quiet voice deep inside you. Teach yourself to be still, a difficult lesson in today's busy world. Relish the symphony of crickets and cicadas on a summer's evening. Enjoy relaxing walks. Notice nature's colors and their combinations in your surroundings. Observe creatures, plants, all of nature. Stop in your tracks and take a careful look. Study a flower. Smile when you hear a bird warble. Marvel at God's creativity. Recognize the complexity, the generous bounty of every species and the unfathomable infiniteness of the universe. See the humor in God's quirkiness. Revel in the majesty of the mountains and the power of the sea. Be intrigued by the mysteries of what you can only imagine. Immerse yourself in simple joys such as aromas, music, and quiet solitude. Daydream. Heighten your consciousness and use your precious senses of touch, smell, sight, hearing and taste. Trust your intuition and instincts.

To expand your creativity you must spend time and nurture it as you would a beautiful garden. The seeds of beauty will not grow otherwise. Consider creativity one of life's priorities.

Why Do We Create Art?

Have you ever thought about the reasons people create art? What is the rationale, the motivation behind making an object of beauty? Why does one choose to paint, sculpt, quilt, draw or compose music? Why does one cook gourmet meals, plant beautiful gardens or design gorgeous jewelry?

After much thought and research, I listed of some of the reasons for creating art:

- Beautify our surroundings
- Stretch the imagination
- Self-fulfillment
- Please ourselves or others
- Provide decoration
- For pure enjoyment and the pleasure of the process
- Healing or therapy
- Celebrate joy
- Give as a gift
- Pass down to future generations
- Share experiences with others
- Draw attention to the ordinary
- Convey spiritual values or beliefs
- Make a statement to the world
- Communicate harmony or unrest to others
- Protest or shock
- For the challenge
- Money, income
- Competition purposes
- An escape or outlet

As I read over this list, all the reasons are relevant to me except "to protest or shock." What are *your* reasons for creating art? What can you add to this list?

Personal Notes

I found one more reason not on the list. It may be the most significant motive of all. From a personal perspective, I simply have no choice. Whether related to art or not, for me to stay happy I *have* to create, something, anything. And I must do it often. For me, creating is a positive, deep, driving urge within. Artistry is just as important for my physical, mental and spiritual wellbeing as the need to eat, sleep and stay warm.

There is a curious aspect I notice in my artistic life. It is how I feel emotionally when I do *not* have the opportunity to create. As a professional fiber art teacher, I'm on the road traveling most of the time. I have little time to create and when I do, it's usually class samples I concentrate on, not the new, exciting quilt that's percolating in my mind, clamoring to come into being. In addition, I watch students in my class play and create as I wish I could. Of course, I am thrilled to see my students having fun with their projects. Yet, there is a certain touch of envy and frustration in me. I wish I could be playing right along with them.

Running in Circles (43˝ in Diameter): *Running in Circles* represents the busyness of my life. Truly, there are days I find myself running around in circles. Made with improvisational circular "blocks."

Creativity

November Moon (37″ × 36″): Melancholy *November Moon*, depicting a grove of bare birch trees in late autumn, is an improvisational quilt based on my interpretation of the drunkard path design. The moon is a collage of metallic lamé fabric, dyed cheesecloth and foil. The leaves are a collage of metallic lamé fabric and polyester sheer organza. Machine quilting is free-motion stitching with metallic copper threads in the design of a tree. *November Moon* detail on opposite page.

When busyness in my life keeps me from creating, I recognize that I am uneasy, restless and at loose ends. I feel thwarted, frustrated, stressed and irritated. For me, it is a necessity to create. Urges and inspirations must come out of my mind and body. If they stay churning and bottled up, the internal flow stops and I feel dammed up inside. To release these negative feelings, I must create, if only to please myself. When I work on what I love (and that is the secret, working on what you love), creativity begins to flow once again and all is right with the world.

Bear in mind we cannot maintain the same level of productivity day after day, year after year. There may be stretches of time when we may feel we have lost our edge or artistic ability. Our inspirational thoughts and drive occasionally take a vacation, a calm time to rest, regenerate and renew our inner being. These unscheduled holidays may occur with complete disregard for timing or our project deadlines. Creativity, like our bodies, needs calm or relaxing downtime before it can continue to function. It is one thing when creativity wants to rest, but quite another when it is alive and in bloom but we don't have or take the time to nurture it. Unfortunately, I feel I never have as much time to make quilts as I wish. I am sure that is also true for most of you as well.

Do you recall times in your artistic journey when your creativity was on vacation and the wellspring within you seemed empty? How long did your dry spells last? Remember, your productivity always comes back in one form or another. It's been my experience it usually returns stronger than ever.

Emotions, Healing and Creativity

Many years ago, when I was a stay-at-home mom with young children, I signed up for an oil painting class at a local craft shop. One of the scenes the class learned to paint was a simple seascape with large boulders on a sandy beach. Enthused with my newfound hobby, I decided on a whim to show my mom and two sisters what I had learned. I spread my paints on the kitchen table and set about playing teacher.

We all started with the identical seascape and the same colors of paint. My oldest sister, who was upset and battling rebellious teens at the time, painted a picture that was a dark tempest, with angry skies and crashing waves. My other sister, calm by nature, painted a serene canvas with long, defined bold strokes and soft colors. My mother's scene evolved entirely different than my sisters'. Seventy at the time, she had trouble holding the paintbrush with her arthritic fingers. Her scene, simple and childlike, included thin wavy lines in the sky representing sea gulls. I'll always remember my amazement at seeing how diversely each one of us painted the same seascape with the identical colors of paint.

Passages of the Spirit (72¼" × 69"): Earthly life is plagued with struggles and human frailties, symbolized in this quilt with somber background colors: red (anger); green (jealousy, hopelessness); gray (anxiety); blue (sadness); and purple (ignorance). The broken, jagged points are discord and conflict. My faith is that in the next life, I'll conquer these failings and my purer spirit will transform into joy, love, hope, serenity and wisdom in the presence of my Creator, represented in gold.

What I learned that day from my students, in this case my family, was a lesson in creativity. One's emotional state of mind plays a major part in the way one creates. It also clearly reveals itself in artwork. Mood and feelings greatly influence not only your design, but also the colors you choose and how you use them. I had no inkling thirty years later, the lesson learned from my family would help define my career in art quilting and my mission and purpose in life.

Emotions and state of mind certainly influence your creativity. When we work from our deepest core and with fervor, we engage a whole range of emotions from past to present life experiences, joyful or sad. The quilts born from our efforts and passion are an emotional extension of us and reflect our feelings. Sometimes blatantly, sometimes subtly, quilts, or any art form, mirror our happiness or heartbreak, exhilaration or despair.

As artists, especially quilters, we often work in solitude on projects for weeks, months, even

Hanging On for Dear Life (23″ × 17″)

years. We enjoy uninterrupted time to think while we work on a project. In my experience, the solitude of the creating process kindles an internal dialogue. This private reflection, as well as the working process, is a form of prayer and healing. For many artists, creating artwork is far more than a craft. It is a comfort, restorative therapy and a spiritual experience. In my lectures I tell my audience much more than mere fabric and threads go into making my quilts. My quilts also include many thoughts of love, joy, sadness, doubt, anxiety and fear, as well as blood, sweat and many tears, literally.

Besides ample time for reflection, there are other therapeutic benefits to quilting. Rhythm quiets and centers the soul. The very nature of quilting is comforting. Consider the cadent sounds of the sewing machine and repetitive actions of hand stitching. Even the simple sensation of touching fabric provides solace and contentment. Young children carry around their security blankets, and grown-up quilters fondle their quilts.

In contrast, art can be harsh therapy during traumatic times. Working from the soul forces us to explore our hidden secrets and innermost feelings and brings them to the forefront of our mind. We may confront emotions and memories that ignite negative feelings. We are forced to acknowledge and face our fears or painful thoughts head on. A threatening scenario for sure, it's one that demands a lot of courage to continue working.

We may suffer a loss of creativity during stressful or grieving times. There are as many ways to heal from grief or difficult experiences as there are people. Everyone has their own way of coping with tough situations. For some, times of personal hardships, challenges or the death of someone dear will directly impact their originality and vision. The loss of creativity can last for many years, even decades. Hurting too much due to personal circumstances, some cannot function artistically. Without enthusiasm or passion, their heart and spirit are just not in it.

For other people, a time of setbacks, loss or hardship is a catalyst for self-expression and the motivation to create. They use their art as a quiet, therapeutic method of healing. By working on their craft they transfer negative emotions from the darkness deep within themselves to the light of day. In other words, their emotions flow from their

Hanging On for Dear Life (Detail): Indeed there are many days I feel as if I am hanging onto my life by only a slim thread.

spirit, mind and body to their artwork. Rather than allowing the stressors to stay bottled up inside, they channel them by creating. The artists feel a sense of relief and freedom. Thus, once painful feelings are released and out in the open, there can be a therapeutic, healing effect.

One student in my class told me she quilted profusely during her mother's illness. Years later, she realized she was creating something pretty to counteract the ugliness in her life during that trying time. She was unconsciously seeking and finding balance by replacing the ugliness with beauty.

Adverse events in one's life such as disappointments, divorce, loneliness, illness or death of a loved one will deplete energy. Creating exudes a positive force that replaces negativity with balance, enabling one to reach equilibrium. The restorative energy flows where it's needed to heal, whether it be the spirit, mind or body. Creating during difficult times does not replenish your energy to your normal level immediately. However, the creative process is beneficial, gradually easing and speeding one's healing and recovery.

Your feelings will not vanish after you make an emotional or healing quilt, nor should you expect an immediate outcome. Healing quilts will not solve issues; they are not a cure-all. Your life's experience will always be a part of you. Once the oppressive emotions, which are imprisoned within you and eat at you like a cancer, are set free, you will feel relief. The pressure or possibly obsession you feel is lifted gradually and healing can begin. The experience and feelings remain but they will not consume you, enabling you to handle negative situations and thoughts more appropriately.

Healing takes more than stitching one quilt. Recovery doesn't happen overnight; it is an ongoing process. And it is only the process that is important. Lose yourself in the journey. Wander. Explore. Discover yourself. Neither the finished work, nor its quality, matters. Through this quest you can achieve renewal, serenity, guidance, balance, harmony, self-awareness, self-esteem and spiritual awakening.

Creativity will have many ups and downs during your lifetime, although the way your creativity reacts to a stressful situation can vary. While your vision may shut down during one stressful time, it may flourish during another.

This is exactly what happened to me. Before my mother's death from cancer in 1981, I was productive artistically, painting portraits and working with sculpture. After her death, sadness and grief took its toll. My creativity was gone, on hiatus for at least ten years. During this grieving period, I played at crafts, but could not function with any enthusiasm. There was an emptiness in my heart.

It wasn't until 1991 when my sister insisted I go with her to a beginning quilting class that my excitement, interest and inspiration in all things artistic returned. My creativity began to revive. However, two years later in 1993 my husband, Denny, was diagnosed with kidney cancer. At the same time, my mother-in-law, Angie, was ill with terminal heart disease and also we were dealing with a rebellious teenager at home. As the old adage states, "When it rains, it pours!" But during this crisis, somehow, I reacted differently, in fact, the exact opposite of the way I did while mourning my mother's death. Grieving the loss of my mother decimated my creativity. But, after my husband's ordeal, my creativity leapt forward and I produced meaningful and symbolic artwork at a rapid pace, such as my healing quilt, *Breaking Point*. Lessons learned from those downtimes and rough periods influenced my quilting and set my career on a new, more productive course.

Recognize and enjoy your downtimes. Be patient. When the time is right and the wellspring of your creative self, heart and spirit are full and refreshed once again, the inspirational thoughts and new ideas will return. Your focus will be on track and life full of color once more.

You do not need to be a Michelangelo to produce a healing quilt. Nor do you need any special talent or training in art. You *do* need the desire to create and focus on your work with passion and sincere desire to heal, but without any expectations. Perhaps you have an inspiration for a quilt design, one that you have thought about making for a while but hesitated to start. It's my experience once you open up your entire being to working on an idea and take a leap of faith, all sorts of things happen, enabling you to move forward and see the quilt to fruition. For this work, stay flexible and do not try to control the outcome. Let the quilt grow and develop as *it* dictates.

When I created *Breaking Point*, I used a pattern I'd designed. If you do not have an idea for a quilt design in mind, another way to encourage recuperative effects of quilting is to make an improvisational quilt. By definition, improvisation is the act of doing something on the spur of the moment and without forethought or planning. When you create this type of quilt, you do so by blending colors, patterns and shapes at your whim, without censure, with no objective in mind, as you work on the project. This can be an effective and eye-opening therapy. More often than not, the quilt takes on a life of its own as the hurtful feelings you hold inside are liberated and flow out of you.

The goal is not to create a visual masterpiece, but to encourage this healing flow. Do not analyze what you are doing or why. Do not make assessments about the work while it is in progress. This is simply a freeing, therapeutic outlet for you. It is important no one, especially yourself, critique this type of work. You cannot and should not judge feelings and emotions. Allow your innermost feelings, emotions or fears to come to life in visual form on a quilt canvas.

When the quilt is completed, take a closer, in-depth look at your project. See if the work offers wisdom or insight into yourself. Consider the colors, fabric selections, patch shapes and how you used these choices, all determined subconsciously and without thought. You may be surprised at what they reveal.

If you are grieving, the colors may be dark and somber because of a sorrowful

Engulfed (42˝ × 76˝): I felt an intense urge to create this work. It wasn't until after the quilt was finished I realized it was symbolic of my current emotional state. I was feeling weary, overburdened and burned out. The hectic schedules and the constant busyness in my life were taking their toll. This quilt provided a sudden insight for me. It was a startling wake-up call to take more time to relax.

heart. There might be jagged lines, expressing discord, personal storms or other unhappy images. Your emotions will manifest in your work, sometimes represented symbolically in the quilt's content, shapes, colors and mood. The opposite is true, as well. If you are happy, your work will reflect that too.

Once the healing process is established and you are feeling less vulnerable, you may wish to reveal your work to trusted friends or possibly show it in a safe venue such as *Sacred Threads* or other similar exhibitions. Or, if the project has served its purpose and you do not want to share, store it away. Some, in a symbolic effort to rid themselves of unpleasant memories, may choose to destroy their piece.

Whether using improvisation or a pattern, your emotions appear, often loud and clear in your artwork. Moreover, you may not even be aware it happens. Such was the case with *Engulfed*. When the inspiration for *Engulfed* hit me, I had a clear vision of how the quilt should look. For the life of me, I couldn't understand the reason why I felt the urge to create *Engulfed*. Most of my quilts are metaphoric in theme or they have a moral or story to teach.

My confusion lasted throughout its construction and completion. About a month later, as I stood in the shower one morning, it finally dawned on me. I identify with trees in many of my quilts, such as *Breaking Point* and *After the Storm*. This quilt was no different. I **was** *Engulfed*. The quilt was a personification. A self-portrait.

I stepped out of the shower, wrapped a towel around myself and went dripping into my studio to take another, more conscious look at my quilt, still hanging on the design board. What I saw was an alarming revelation. If this tree was a characterization of me, then stress was more prevalent in my life and taking a greater toll than I realized. Not only did the quilt reveal volumes about my anxious, troubled state of mind, but also how emotions manifest in artwork.

First, I noticed the dark, somber colors of the tree. Using all dark and dreary colors can be a sign of depression. Literally, it denotes lack of color in one's life. I saw the tree burning with flames licking around the base of its trunk. Fire has many meanings. It can be either good or harmful. A comfort or devastation. In the context of *Engulfed*,

I interpreted the licking flames as destructive and chaotic. I recognized the tree's message to me. I was burning myself out.

Next, I saw the tree's posture and body language, an unspoken and subconscious form of communication. The tree was bent considerably, as if laden and bearing the weight of the world. During the time I designed and constructed *Engulfed*, I was working hard and overwhelmed with the busyness in my life. I was exhausted. The tree matched my mood exactly. I quickly decided I was in serious need of a vacation.

Yes, my quilt exposed my emotional state. But, an even more startling eye-opener for me was how I subconsciously incorporated my negative emotions into the design and colors of my work. During the planning and construction of *Engulfed*, I was completely unaware of any unusual emotional influences.

The lesson learned from *Engulfed* echoed what I learned years ago when I held the painting session with my family; emotions *do* play a major part in designs and color choices whether one realizes it or not.

There is an epilogue to this story. A few months later that same year, my family went on vacation to Bryce Canyon National Park in Utah. As we were hiking around a bend on the canyon rim, I came upon a tree, an exact replica of *Engulfed*. Severely burned from a forest fire, the tree had the same body language and was hanging dangerously close to the canyon's edge. I'm sure other hikers wondered about my sanity as I proceeded to take three rolls of 36-exposure slide film of

Tree from Bryce Canyon National Park, Utah

this one tree. A few years later, I returned to the park and the tree still stood, steadfast and clinging to the cliff. I took more photographs. No doubt, the tree is listed now as one of the most photographed trees in the park. In this instance, I constructed the quilt first and then saw the inspiration. Had I known about the Utah tree and emotional influences ahead of time, I'd have titled the quilt *Over the Edge*. A bit more fitting, don't you think?

Inspirations

However you name them…inspirations, visions, ideas, brainstorms, insights… we all have them. They are part of the creativity that blesses us in our everyday lives. These thoughts are stimuli urging us to be productive not only in art, but in every facet of life. Inspiration spurs us to create fresh works, solve problems and excite us with original artistic techniques and designs.

You are the vehicle for these inspirations. Do you focus only on the rocks and obstacles in the road ahead, or do you keep the pathway open to new ideas? Do you welcome inspirations or ignore and make excuses why you can't or won't act on them? Do you recognize a creative thought when it occurs and are you receptive and open-minded to it? Are you willing to be an instrument, bringing your images to fruition?

Personal Notes

Not all inspirations are created equal. Some are brilliant and life changing. Some are exciting. Others may not be worth further exploration after a bit of reflection. Another may frighten or make you wary of starting a project. A few will cause you to hesitate or balk. Some you may reject. I've been blessed with many creative visions and ideas in my artistic life, and they are all of the above.

The inspiration for *Breaking Point* changed my life and also my husband's. I consider the vision for *Creation of the Sun and Stars* to be a divine gift and am forever grateful I am the quilter chosen to give it life. I was passionate about the vision for *Portrait of My Soul*. When the thought came to me in church that evening, I was motivated and started the quilt immediately with newfound enthusiasm.

On the other hand, I hesitated about another inspiration that also materialized during a church service. As with *Portrait of My Soul*, again I must admit I was daydreaming and not listening to the sermon. Completely unrelated to the church service that night, an inspiration came to me. The notion of a quilt depicting a theme of life after death nudged the corners of my imagination. I envisioned a design for the quilt, but hesitated even to consider making it because I worried the subject matter was too depressing and morbid. I feared a quilt with such a topic might upset those who viewed it. Ultimately and after much soul-searching, I relented. As I believe creativity and inspiration come from the Divine, I decided to trust in my vision and began planning *Life Beyond*, based on a scene at nearby Blacklick Woods Metro Park. I allowed the quilt to take on a life of its own as I constructed it. Rather than being gloomy as I feared, the completed quilt portrays optimism and hope. The quilt has been well-received and to this day remains a viewer favorite.

Life Beyond (62˝ × 86˝): Winter at the pond in Blacklick Woods, a nearby metro park, is the inspiration for *Life Beyond*. Although the season is associated with death of living things, life beyond what we are able to see still exists. I believe there will be life beyond my "winter," too. The absence of a horizon in the scene's background symbolizes infinity. On the surface everything at the pond seems dead, but if you look closely, you can see life in the quilt… goldfish swimming under the ice.

Many times, we reject, either deliberately or unconsciously, the inspirations that come our way. When hit with the idea to begin the *Sacred Threads Exhibition*, I balked and outright refused to accept it, at least for a while. I made every excuse why I couldn't or shouldn't take action.

Inspirational Images for **Life Beyond**: Clockwise from top left: fish in ice; winter scene; leaf in ice; and detail of *Life Beyond.*

I believe there are three parts to an inspiration. First, the creative thought or idea comes to mind. Next, the thought is followed closely by an initial emotional reaction, which may be positive, negative or indifferent. In my personal experience, I find a third aspect to inspiration, what my inner voice, my spiritual self, thinks about the idea. The creative thought and emotional reaction come from the mind. The spiritual aspect comes from the heart.

When facing a dilemma, two questions I ask myself are, "Will this idea (or quilt) be beneficial and inspire others? Will it give joy, comfort or healing?" If the answer to either of these questions is yes, I've learned to trust in my inner feelings and found it is wondrous to follow my artistic inspirations, even ones that do not appeal to me at first. I create because I consider it is my calling and inspirations are gifts to me. I always try to be open and willing. It's not always easy to say yes and be willing.

For example, in the early planning days of *Sacred Threads*, I asked myself why I was the one chosen to found this show. Me, someone without experience organizing events or raising money. How was I supposed to put on such a major production? The one answer I could settle on…I was the only person foolish enough to say yes. Yet, I've never regretted following through with my inspirations, even those I didn't want to accept.

So when do inspirations happen? You never know when or where a great idea will hit you. Almost guaranteed, it will be when you least expect it. I seldom ever have creative thoughts when I am stressed, busy, worried or overly tired. Most inspirations occur when I'm quiet and in a relaxed state. During these times the mind and spirit are receptive to new ideas. As I believe these precious revelations come from a higher source, this is no surprise. We can hear God best when our minds and bodies are still and our surroundings relaxed and peaceful.

Many of my breakthroughs come during twilight sleep. That is the period of time just as you are drifting off to sleep at night or dozing in and out of wakefulness in the early morning hours just before arising for the new day. I've also had flashes of creative insight come to me in church, outdoors in nature settings, in the shower, interacting with other artists or kindred spirits and even walking up the stairs. The keys to their timing seem to be quiet, relaxation and mental receptiveness.

Do you recognize the moment when innovative thinking springs into *your* head? Many of us are so involved with day-to-day activities, health and family issues and distractions too numerous to mention, that even when we do experience creative vision, we don't perceive it as such. We are not attentive to the moment. An idea may fly right by our mind's eye without as much as a sideways glance; we are too focused on the busywork and concerns of our day. I am guilty of this as well.

I'm making a strong effort these days to be more alert to my thoughts and actions. Staying focused on the task at hand and not letting my mind wander is a serious challenge for me, perhaps one of the most difficult resolutions I've ever made. Rather than concentrate on the job in front of me, I ponder what I did yesterday or mull over what I need to do tomorrow. Also, I tend to worry, am anxious and often am concerned over trivial matters. It is not easy to overcome these brain-numbing, energy-wasting habits when you've done it for most of your life. I'm counting on my persistence to pull me through this challenge.

Once you are perceptive to your creative thoughts, take action to ensure you remember them. Inspirations are fleeting. It is easy to forget them without a written reminder. Even though it may be inconvenient, take the time to jot down ideas that pop into your mind as soon as possible. Keep a notebook, journal or even just paper and pencil with you at all times, even by your bedside. Make a quick sketch of a design, describe the colors you envision or record any other details from your

Summer's Bounty (30˝ in Diameter): This quilt is inspired by one of nature's favorite wildflowers, the sunflower, which blooms profusely in mid to late summer.

inspiration. Store all this information in one special file so your ideas are organized and easy to find when you want to refer back to them. You might also consider keeping a scrapbook of magazine or newspaper clippings, postcards, color combinations or items that spark your creative interest as a reference and resource for future designs or projects.

Until now, we've talked about inspiration in terms of creative thought or ideas. But inspiration also means to be stimulated or motivated by some thing or person. What excites you? For me, mainly it's love of nature. I'm forever enamored with beauty that surrounds me when I am outdoors. The splendor of nature energizes and nurtures my spirituality and imagination. When I'm one with nature, I am at peace. If I receive an intuitive thought that touches my heart, often I see it as a metaphor between nature and life. Examples are *Breaking Point*, *Against All Odds* and *Life Beyond*.

Perhaps there is a special person who inspires you, and not necessarily from a creative standpoint. I made my own list of the top influential people in my life. Some are living, some not. Although possessing completely different personalities, they share some characteristics in common:

- Fun and enjoyable to be with, they have a sense of humor and we laugh together.
- They are upbeat and optimistic about life, even during adverse times.
- While not necessarily embracing a religion, they have a spiritualness about them.
- They are honest and down to earth in their views.
- Treating others with dignity, kindness and respect is important to them.

Most of those on my list are not artists, but friends or family. Still, they are an inspiration for me to be creative. Being around them makes me happy, relaxed and comfortable, all of which one needs to feed the creative spirit. Who is on your list? Who inspires you and why? Take a moment now to reflect.

Personal Notes

Once you have thought about who strengthens and encourages you, ask yourself two insightful questions, "Am I an inspiration to others?" and "Is my artwork of value and enlightening to others?" Remember, being an inspiration to others is being an inspiration to yourself.

Design Walls

Many artists and quilters use a design wall. Any empty wall in your home will do. Its purpose is to pin your work or quilt blocks in an upright position so you can view the project during the construction process. This allows you a better perspective of colors and design elements. Building a design wall can be as simple as tacking a large piece of flannel, batting or felt to the wall. You could substitute a large corkboard or bulletin board and use pins to secure the project. For something more permanent, you can nail an unpainted sheet of wallboard to a wall in your workspace.

In all my classes and workshops I ask my students if they use a design wall when they are working on a quilting project. It doesn't matter whether one is constructing traditional or contemporary quilts, or another art medium. A design wall is perhaps the most important, least used and under-appreciated item in your studio.

Pin your project to a design wall, stand back at least ten feet and observe your progress with objectivity. This will help you see which design and color choices please you, and which do not. Working on a design wall enables you to make the best decisions quickly and easily as you construct a quilt. Stand away from your work and you'll know instantly whether a quilt has enough color and value (light to dark) contrast and striking visual impact.

I explain to my students art is all about illusion. They must exaggerate colors and values in order for objects to appear dimensional. When you work with contrasts, colors, designs, lines and values, the most important elements in art, you cannot fully appreciate the way all these visuals work together if you stand too close. Colors or values appearing to have sufficient contrast when they are 12"-18" from your eyes may blend together or wash out when viewed from a distance of ten feet. Without contrasts there is no visual impact for the viewer. Think about quilts you see displayed from across a crowded room at quilt shows, the ones that catch your attention and call your name. Those are the quilts with impact, intensity, plenty of color and contrasts.

We can view our own personal lives from a design wall as well. I discovered this one day after class as one of my students and I were discussing a variety of subjects. She asked me what influenced my quilting career. I explained that after my husband, Denny, had an operation to remove a cancerous tumor in his kidney, I wanted to make a healing quilt. During this time we experienced turmoil and struggled with anxiety and fear. But, looking back a few years after this crisis, I was amazed to see how my husband's cancer, an unexpected detour in our marriage, had changed our lives in a positive way.

In fact, the wonderful career in quilting and teaching I now enjoy is a direct result of what we endured with Denny's illness. Deeply involved in his health problems, with our vision obscured by emotions, we didn't…couldn't…see the whole picture during that turbulent time. I liken that situation to my ground fog analogy: When you are driving in fog, the road is still beneath your wheels, but the road ahead is obscured. Caught up in the fear and anxiety of the moment, you can't see the path that guides you and are afraid to trust the road is still there. So it was with us. Caught up in the fog of his illness, it was hard for us to trust the road we were traveling could lead us to a happy future.

Though impossible to appreciate at the time, Denny's illness had a silver lining. The problems we faced and overcame taught us valuable lessons. We learned life is precious and one must live it to the fullest. We also learned what is truly important. His cancer influenced not only my career decisions, but my art and quilts as well. It changed us for the better. In retrospect, his cancer was a blessing in disguise. This insight became clear to me when I observed the circumstances from the distance of several years later and with emotional detachment. Only now can I understand the good that emerged from that bad experience.

Later in the same conversation with my student, we were discussing *Sacred Threads*, the quilt exhibition I founded. Anxious and worried about taking on such a huge endeavor, I wanted no part of starting this exhibit although the inspiration to do so was strongly pushing me forward.

I told my student how everything began to fall into place for the show, and how wonder and amazement filled me as I watched it all unfold. I told her it was as if I were standing on the outside looking through a window at my concerns. I would stand back and consider all the issues causing my anxiety: the funding, the venue, gathering volunteers and

At Sea (36˝ × 28˝): Inspired by ocean waves.

committee members who would work with me to make this show the incredible exhibit it is. From my viewpoint behind the glass, I could observe how these worrisome issues were being answered clearly and effortlessly. The show was destined to be. With this insight, I was reassured.

It was at that moment I stopped talking to my student, acutely aware of the analogy I'd just recognized between two design walls…one wall where I observed and made decisions about my quilts…and another where I observed and found solutions relevant to what was happening in my life. I began to see my life from a different perspective.

You cannot make appropriate design and color decisions when you are too close in proximity to the work. This same concept applies to other areas in our lives as well. Just as with art and quilting, we need a design wall in our lives. We cannot make crucial decisions and appropriate choices if we are looking at the dilemma from a vantage point that is too close. Pin up the problem or situation on life's design wall, step away and observe it from a distance. Do so with complete detachment and without emotions clouding your judgment. As with our quilts, rather than focusing on fragments, we will have a better perspective and be able to see the entire picture before making choices that will impact the fabric of our lives.

A Tree of Many Colors

Did you notice the colors of the tree trunk in *Promise of Spring*? I included every color of the rainbow into the trunk. Would you have used all those colors in your tree? Why not?

As an artist, you should not limit yourself with self-imposed boundaries. You may paint or create what you are able to see, but why restrict yourself to reproducing only what the human eye can behold? Strive to envision and interpret what you cannot readily see. An artist should "paint" with imagination, not just what he or she perceives as reality.

Many times I feel I am in my own little world when I create. I must admit I like it there. My world is one of make-believe. I play. I imagine. I pretend. There are no rules, and everything can and does exist at my whim. It is said that imitation is the sincerest form of flattery. When I create I have an opportunity to imitate the Creator. Whether designing a complete scene, an object or a detail, I often think to myself, "If I could be the Creator, this is how I'd make it." I find these thoughts liberating and an act of worship for me.

Promise of Spring (Detail; full Size 62″ x 73″): As a gentle spring breeze dances across Blacklick Pond, it coaxes the promise of new life from the branches of the weeping willow. The *Promise of Spring* represents the reawakening and rebirth of earthly life after winter. *"Promise"* also celebrates the remembrance of life...life that has ceased to exist in our world, symbolized by the quilted ghost branches, leaves and flowers, but revives after death in the life beyond.

I made this quilt entirely with improvisational techniques. It started from a single oval block and rapidly took on a life of its own, growing in all directions. It is a perfect example of how creativity flows and turns inspiration into an artwork with a purpose to touch the spirit of others.

In my world, I believe everything my eyes see actually contains all colors. Because I'm limited in my human vision, I am only able to see an object's primary color depending on how light refracts or bounces off its matter or substance at any given time.

I do not know if my theory about color is scientific fact in the study of physics. While awed and fascinated by science, my brain is challenged by the abstract theories and math connected with it. I can only appreciate and enjoy it. My personal belief about color is the way it is in my imagination, in my gut and in what I've observed.

My concept of color is due in part to a Sweetgum tree that grew in our backyard for many years. I loved that tree with its

star-shaped leaves and rough bark. Every autumn it was a sight to behold. The green leaves would start to turn in October. Each leaf would turn first to a beautiful yellow. Then, in sequence, the yellow leaf would morph to yellow-orange, then to orange, red-orange, red, maroon,

A sweet gum tree of many colors in our backyard (above) and **Promise of Spring** details (pages 124 and 125).

Creativity 125

to finally burgundy before it danced to the ground. Each leaf changed at its own leisurely pace. The tree was robed in a myriad of colors during the autumn season. I realized the tree contained all those colors within itself. The pigments within the leaves were always there; it was just that I couldn't observe them until the timing was right.

As another example, when we envision sky we automatically think blue. Of course, the space we perceive as sky appears blue, most of the time. How many colors of blue do you see during the course of a day, from dawn to dusk, or in distance, from the horizon to directly over your head?

Think of how many *other* colors you see in the sky, every imaginable tint, combination and color of yellow, peach, lavender, green, orange and red at sunrise and sunset. Nature provides thousands of colors of gray during rainstorms, dark navy to black at night. I've even seen the sky a sickly olive green just before a tornado warning. The sky can be any color you can conceive.

I constructed the tree trunk in *Promise of Spring* using my color philosophy. I truly

(Left and center) Violet mushrooms and a bush with each leaf a different color were scenes we photographed in Australia; striped trees on a California beach (right).

These examples of nature's vivid imagination should inspire artists to create with abandon.

believe that tree trunks contain a multitude of colors, the ones we see as well as the ones we do not. In my world, tree bark isn't just brown. So I included *all* colors of fabric when I made the quilt: purple, navy, rust, deep green, maroon, orange. Name it and it's in there.

In my travels I love to take photos of unusual objects and scenes, especially if they are colorful or a hue out of the norm for me. Flowers, trees, insects all come in astonishing colors.

I photographed these three colorful snails within a few yards of each other in Møns Klint Nature Preserve in Denmark. While shopping at the Queen Victoria Market in Melbourne, Australia, Denny and I discovered the whimsical dragon fruit. In contrast to its bold fuchsia and lime green colors, it has a subtle, delicate taste.

Creativity

Snails, each a different color...orange, blue or yellow...live within a few yards of each other in the Møns Klint landmark and nature reserve in Denmark. These steep, beautiful sea cliffs are on the island of Møn in the Baltic Sea and they are 143 meters (469 feet) high and are made of white chalk.

I've seen striped trees on a California beach, an Australian bush with each leaf a different hue, plants with solid black leaves, violet mushrooms and dramatically exotic fruit. Quirkiness abounds in our natural world. Be free to explore *your* artistic license and creativity. Don't limit yourself to reproducing only the realism you know. Depict not what is, but what you *imagine* it might be. Dream and have fun! Design work and choose colors that intrigue the spirit and stir the imagination.

Valley of Fire (Detail; full size 44˝ x 33˝): The Valley of Fire State Park in Nevada is the inspiration for this quilt. Though Lake Mead is located miles from the park, I decided to make a desert collage and include the lake in my scene. As artists, we have no restrictions. We have freedom not only to create what we can see, but what we imagine.

The Spider's Web

It is said you cannot imagine anything that doesn't already exist, and I believe it to be true. I've created something in my artwork from imagination and thought to myself, "This certainly isn't realistic," only to discover later it certainly did exist in nature.

For example, after I completed the quilt top for *The Spider's Web*, I thought it would be fun to add a fuzzy texture to the tree limbs. I decided the best way to do this was to utilize a medley of unusual threads, applied to the branches.

I freely stitched the threads, yarns and wooly fibers in a random, loosely intertwined hodgepodge pattern onto water-soluble stabilizer. I deliberately left open spaces in the tangle of thread so the fabrics on the quilt's surface would show through. Once the stabilizer melted away with warm water, a colorful, lacy web of thread remained. I free-motion stitched the web of thread onto the surface of all the tree's branches.

I designed this quilt with two openings between the branches. To enhance the piece, a spider's web spans the larger opening. By using a rectangular wooden frame from an old art canvas, minus the canvas fabric, as a makeshift loom, I created a free-form, hand-woven contemporary lace. Knotted macramé-style, with many different yarns, alpaca wools and thick threads, the lace became my "spider web." As with a real web suspended from a tree or bush, the support lines of my web were inserted between the quilt top and backing fabric, allowing the lace to hang freely.

Once finished, the quilt resembled a tree one imagines to exist only in fairy tales. Not realistic as far as I knew or had ever seen, but I thought it interesting and fun to make. Years later, when my teaching travels took me to New Zealand, I discovered my imaginary tree does exist.

We arrived in New Zealand ten days early to vacation and explore this wonderful country. We traveled to Te Anu, a small, remote town located almost at the bottom of the south island. From there we began our overnight trip into Doubtful Sound and the Tasman Sea.

When you are at Doubtful Sound, you truly believe you are at the very ends of the earth. And you are, literally. It is perhaps the most beautiful, serene setting on this planet.

The Spider's Web (43˝ × 39˝): Using wooly threads for texture on the surface branches of *The Spider's Web*, this quilt was fantasy from my imagination, or so I thought.

To reach Doubtful Sound, you must first cross a large lake by boat, then cross over a mountain pass by bus before finally descending into a fjord where you board a boat for an overnight experience in Doubtful Sound. At the mountain pass we went through

Details from **The Spider's Web**: Clockwise from top left: thread texture on a branch; handmade web created using a variety of threads in varying thicknesses; embroidered spider as a disguise.

While finishing this quilt, I accidently poked a hole in the backing fabric. To cover my mistake, I closed the puncture with stitches to secure it, and then embroidered a spider over the flaw to hide my mistake. This solution was a perfect fit with the quilt's theme.

Our errors often challenge us. Consider them as opportunities to be creative. Don't you love the beady green eyes?

Creativity

a dark, magical woodland. The imaginary tree I'd envisioned and created, *The Spider's Web*, exists and thrives in this corner of the earth. The scene before me was surreal. All the trees were heavily draped with strands of moss and their limbs coated with thick, fuzzy lichen, just like the texture on my quilt's branches. I was in an enchanted forest and expected to see trolls and fairies peek from behind the trees at any moment.

The Sequence of Creativity

Over the course of many years and art mediums, I've observed a definite pattern and progression of emotions during the creative process, no matter what art form or project I happened to be working on at that time, whether painting, sculpting or quilting. I call it my sequence of creativity.

Breaking dawn on Doubtful Sound and the Tasman Sea in New Zealand.

For me it always follows the same pattern:

1. When I first begin the project, I am enthusiastic, thrilled with my work and excited with the progress I'm making. I am absolutely sure this will be one of my best works.

2. As my art piece grows, so do my doubts. I still feel inspired, but am now a bit more reserved, unsettled. Perhaps this quilt may not develop as well as I visualized or hoped.

3. As the end of the project approaches, I have serious qualms. It's not turning out as planned and I'm certain I could have done better work. I fear the piece won't be well-received by others. Is it even worth finishing, I wonder?

4. Anxious and impatient to finish the work, I hate what I've done. It's not worthy and probably my worst quilt ever. I really don't want to look at it anymore.

5. Now it's been about six months since I've finished the project. When I look at it anew, I tell myself, "It doesn't look so bad, I guess. Others seem to like it. Maybe it's not as awful as I thought."

6. A year or two later, I look at the quilt again in a whole new light. I think to myself, "Wow! This quilt looks pretty good. Did I actually create this? How did I accomplish what I did?"

I experience this same succession of emotions and thoughts with every project I've made and in every art form.

I believe this sequence is common and normal for creative spirits. All humans, especially artists, deal with insecurities and misgivings. We wonder how others will judge our art and us. Our doubts and fears gain a foothold in our minds and our creativity suffers. We lose the carefree joy and enthusiasm that is so vital in the artistic

process. We also run the risk of something even worse. If we listen to the negative thoughts crowding our minds, we may either not finish our project or refuse to share our work because we are too self-conscious. We think it's not good enough.

Awareness is a wonderful eye-opener to understanding yourself. Take a few moments to think about my creativity sequence. Does this pattern seem familiar to you? Is this how you perceive your artwork while constructing it?

What do *you* experience when you create? Do you have unfinished projects stuffed away? Do you have work you won't show to anyone, even when you finish it?

Personal Notes

Log Cabin Images: A Study in Copper (25˝ × 68˝): This fun quilt depicts my improvisational interpretation of a log cabin block design.

The centers of each block are patches of copper lamé fabric, as is the zigzag copper strip down the length of the quilt. The copper strip is pleated. Small, folded strips and wedges created from other fabrics in the quilt are inserted into the bodies of the pleats for color balance and harmony. The turquoise strips are cotton fabric embellished with curly lines of gold foiling and overlaid with polyester sheer organza.

Many times, we tend to think we are alone in our circumstances; what we feel or experience is rare and no one else has obstacles as daunting as ours. Knowing this same sequence happens to others is both a comfort and a relief. We can learn another important secret to nurturing our creativity from this as well. Realizing it is a common pattern, we must learn to ignore the negative thoughts threatening our creative spirit, our capabilities, our inspirations, our work and belief in ourselves. Be cognizant when these undesirable feelings occur. Disregard them! Do not let them sway you from your course.

Take notice of your feelings as you work on your next project and record your thoughts and sentiments in your journal. If you are plagued with negative emotions during the creative process, do you recognize them as a problem? Many times, being mindful and alert to a situation or problem while it is occurring enables you to handle it with more ease and find the solutions you are seeking.

Critique Verses Criticism

No one likes to be criticized. Words of criticism are a negative force, usually delivered with a mean intent. Criticism delivered in such a manner tears us down. It is not constructive nor does it offer any suggestions for improvement. Our common response is to return in kind; our reaction to criticism is usually negative, unhappy and defensive.

However, almost all artists can benefit greatly from critique. Indeed, critique is beneficial for our creativity. Critique is positive, supportive and upbeat. It offers a different viewpoint, useful suggestions, new possibilities and potential options to improve a project.

Sometimes we become fixated on a detail or come to an impasse regarding the entire project. We are jammed. At a loss, we know instinctively something is wrong, but are unsure how to fix the problem. At a dead end, we don't know what to do next.

When stumped by problems such as these, don't hesitate to ask a trusted friend for positive feedback. A fresh pair of eyes to locate trouble spots is extremely helpful. Choose someone with whom you can brainstorm and bounce ideas back and forth. Worthwhile critique from another artist, friend or relative can help us determine what

We all need to understand the distinction between criticism (negative) and critique (constructive). Distinguish the emotional undertones between the two and recognize the spirit in which it's intended. Do not dwell on criticism of yourself or your art from negative people or take it to heart. More importantly, do *not* criticize yourself. Criticism destroys your creative spirit; a constructive critique will enlighten it.

is missing in our work. He or she may come up with suggestions or solutions allowing us to enhance, continue and finish our piece. Their helpful comments may deliver the breakthrough "AHA!" moment we are seeking.

Learn to be open to those offering well-meaning, positive suggestions without becoming defensive. Listen. Consider their suggestions with an open mind. Decide for yourself which suggestions have merit and those that won't work for you.

It is imperative to separate yourself emotionally from your artwork or project if you do ask for feedback or critique. Do not take critique personally. Some people take advice or suggestions as a personal affront, even ideas that are valid and intended to be supportive. They automatically assume the one offering a critique is finding fault. If you find yourself over-reacting like this, please remember that all artists need and improve from beneficial feedback.

Art is a journey and no one knows the exact route. If one offers advice with honesty, good intentions and gentleness of spirit, at the very least listen and consider if you can learn anything from the advice offered. For a productive critique, it is important

Firestorm (38˝ × 36˝): Completely improvisational, *Firestorm* represents my interpretation of irregular, triangular log cabin "blocks."

to choose a person who will give you an honest assessment. You need critique from someone who tells you the truth, not what you want to hear or what spares your feelings. I advise you find and surround yourself with positive people whose opinions you trust and respect.

My sister, Augustine Ellis, excels at writing. When I was writing my book, *Quilting by Improvisation* (DragonThreads 2006), she proofread my chapters. She was my main copy editor. One chapter in particular gave me trouble, the one on manipulations. She insisted I rewrite that chapter over and over, what seemed like a dozen times. I would groan in dismay, but she always offered helpful critiques and suggestions. I could see at the time the points she made were right on target. Nonetheless, I was frustrated and it was a grueling task to revise the chapter so many times. To this day, I get compliments on my book for being so concise and clearly written. I always give credit to both my sister and myself...my sister, for seeing the trouble spots in my book and urging me to amend it repeatedly until it was right, and to myself for having the good sense to listen to her.

Finding a Good Support System

As I wrote above, my sister, Augustine, was instrumental in helping me write *Quilting by Improvisation*. She has been one of the key players in my support system during my quilting career, along with my husband, Denny, and others.

A support system is a group of people who are your advocates. They believe in you. They encourage you. They advise you with constructive feedback and help you work through problems. They do not criticize, hinder or compete with you. It is not only necessary, but crucial for us to have a good support system.

The persons in your support network can be family, friends, other artists or someone with whom you share a common ground. Above all, the one adjective that should describe your supporter is positive, positive, POSITIVE! An affirmative attitude inspires not only you, but your creativity and motivation. Your advocate should be upbeat, a person you look forward to seeing and enjoy being around. Your advocate should be someone you hold in high esteem, and one who respects you, your work, your ideas and your purpose. Your supporter should enhance you. By the same token, you must return the favor. Be his or her champion as well. It is a mutual give and take. We must help each other evolve and grow.

Sources of support, comfort and camaraderie include guilds, bees or gatherings of like-minded artists. As quilters, we bind our quilts, but quilts bind us together in return.

Some people completely isolate themselves in their studios for long periods of time or work without interaction or contact with other artists. I believe this self-imposed isolation is unhealthy. We are social creatures and need to connect with other kindred spirits for inspiration, encouragement and advice.

We all need a sense of belonging, a feeling of connectedness. Relating to others through our artwork generates creative energy. This energy, which flows back and forth among those involved, invigorates and feeds our souls. We can share techniques and ideas, or a quilt's comforting or healing message.

Poppies (Detail)

Realize there is a difference between isolation and enjoying periods of solitude. While I appreciate the quiet solitude of working alone without distractions in my studio, I feel unsettled if I do not interact with others. I am definitely more productive when I am connected or talk with someone during my workday. Also, I find I stay more motivated, focused and enthused about art when interacting with other creative beings. But as with all things in life, balance is the key to success. Too much contact becomes distracting and counter-productive.

Close interaction with others has another advantage…reassurance. Have you ever

exclaimed to a friend, "I thought *I* was the only one!" after she confided in you about a predicament she was going through? There are times when I am troubled about something in my art, be it teaching or another situation, and feel as if I am the only one in the world who has this particular problem. If I keep these thoughts to myself, I tend to dwell on the difficulty even more. The problem takes on a life of its own, energizes and magnifies, appearing worse than it really is. As it grows into a catastrophe, I become more anxious and frightened.

On the other hand, when I share my perplexing situation with others, I am comforted. The problem does not loom as large or threatening. During the conversation, I am reminded once again we

Poppies (32˝ × 19½˝): A friend and I decided to sneak away for a week and enjoy a "quilter's retreat." No husbands, cooking or cleaning…just relaxing and working without interruptions. During those glorious days, I made *Poppies*, an improvisational raw edge quilt, completed in three days. I've never had more fun making a piece of artwork. We swapped fabric and offered encouragement to each other. When one interacts with other artists, creativity blooms and prospers.

Creativity

share a common bond of similar problems. I understand others face the same quandaries as I do.

The knowledge I'm not alone lessens the feeling of isolation. The challenge doesn't disappear but, somehow, I can deal with it more easily. Lesson learned: Share your problems with a trusted friend. All people face a common thread of problems and dilemmas in life.

The Art of Gratitude

Studies indicate that gratitude is a positive, powerful emotion, one that has a significant impact on our wellbeing. Those who research the subject say people who are grateful are happier in general, less depressed during trying times and respond better socially with others. Also, they are more optimistic, less stressed and more creative.

I heartily agree with these studies. I know from personal experience when I feel truly grateful, my entire demeanor and mental attitude change for the better. I am more optimistic and less stressed. My creativity and productivity increase. I definitely am happier with myself and those around me.

Think about gratitude from a personal viewpoint. If you give someone a gift of value or your time and the recipient does not respond or express thanks, how do you feel? Probably hurt or angry. Chances are you may not give that person another gift. On the other hand, if the recipient acknowledges your gift with sincere, heartfelt appreciation, how do you feel? Of course, you feel happy and even more generous. Everyone wants to feel cherished for who we are and what we do.

I make it a practice to think about everything I am grateful for when I pray. One of my private observations is that as human parents, we are hurt or unhappy when we lavish our children with love, gifts, attention or our precious time and they do not respond to our caring gestures nor seem to appreciate what we do for them. However, if we see they are grateful, we are inclined to do even more for our children. So it is, I believe, with our spiritual Father, who luckily for us has more love and patience than we do.

Two secrets to appreciative thinking are mindfulness and habit. I find when I am attentive to my surroundings, I tend to relax more, smile more and take more pleasure in small, everyday happenings. For instance, as I was writing these very words, a heavy thunderstorm blew through, indeed a rare occurrence in late December for central Ohio. I love thunderstorms. There is something primitive and cleansing about them that speaks to me and gives me deep pleasure. I stopped writing until the storm passed. Instead, I gazed out the window, smiling and listening to the rain and thunder, grateful to be a witness to this unusual event.

For most of us, day-to-day life is dictated by our routines. New resolutions that seem difficult to

Windows (18″ × 38″): Created using my improvisational techniques, *Windows* features three freeform blocks, each with an open center. Webs of various threads span the holes.

Free-motion quilted in a jagged motif.

Creativity   143

achieve at first become easier with practice. In other words, they become a regular habit. Why not, then, make it a daily practice to be grateful for all the good things in our lives? One way to get into the habit of gratitude is logging in your journal. Every day, or as often as possible, jot down what you are grateful for. Writing the words on paper gives energy to your feelings.

Don't save your appreciation only for happy events or milestones. Look for joy in the small blessings. Possibly it's a beloved pet or wild birds at the feeder whose antics make you grin, or a beautiful plant that blooms and gives you pleasure (I always smile when my orchids bloom.) Some days when everything goes wrong, it's hard to find anything to be thankful for. Then I dig a little deeper. It could be I am grateful the sun is *finally* shining in Ohio, I didn't gain weight that morning despite the sundae I ate the night before, or searching through my stash, I found the perfect fabric for my quilt.

Remember, every situation, action or thought in your life has both negative and positive aspects. It's the yin/yang of our existence. Always choose the positive outlook and be grateful. All the small thanksgivings you extend into the universe accumulate. The result is a happy, optimistic state of mind.

It may be difficult to maintain an appreciative mindset when one is challenged with problems or difficult periods in life. No matter how serious the issue, I am painfully aware I tend to focus inwardly when stressed or upset. Almost always, the emphasis is negative. My attention focuses on what is wrong or lacking in my life, *not* what is right and abundant. Since negativity begets even more negativity, the results are additional unpleasant feelings and an emotional downward spiral.

At this point, the "design wall" approach may help. Once my narrow field of vision widens to encompass the entire, clearer picture at an emotional distance, there is a shift in attitude. The focus changes from an inward to an outward viewpoint that usually includes others. From the bigger perspective comes a better insight into the problem. The situation may remain unchanged, but my understanding may improve. With understanding comes acceptance. With acceptance, gratitude can grow once more.

Every day I give thanks for the privilege of creating and teaching art. I am truly grateful for my family and friends who are always there to support and nurture me. I have only the deepest respect and admiration for my students. We are on both life and artistic journeys, and I am forever thankful our paths cross in the classroom. My students are an invaluable treasure trove of inspiration and joy for me. I've benefited from their creativity, humor, questions, suggestions and comments in class and during lectures. I gather knowledge, insights and understanding from them. I always try to be open to learning; there is so much left to learn in my life. I eagerly look forward to the future, where I will gain more wisdom from the wonderful art of quilting.

Passages of the Spirit (Detail)

As This Book Comes to an End...

It seems fitting to echo the same words I wrote in my Introduction. I love being an artist and a teacher. I feel my calling is to inspire others with my artwork, in the classroom or through my lectures. My quest is to encourage, motivate and help my students. By creating their own original works of art, they may achieve self-expression, self-discovery and self-confidence.

Some years ago, I came to the realization I am where God wants me to be. I am fortunate beyond words. I know the work I do, creating, teaching and speaking, is the mission in my life and I am forever grateful. Many never recognize nor accept their true calling. I find serenity knowing through my art, I am an instrument for the Divine.

I remember as a young child, I dreamt of traveling around the world and my dream came true. I teach internationally and travel all over the globe. As a little girl, I was too shy to raise my hand in school. Today, I am a public speaker. As a teen, I all but failed sewing in junior high school. Now, I teach quilting classes and have authored three books. I didn't learn to quilt until I was in my early forties nor realize quilting was my purpose in life until my early fifties. When I consider how my life has evolved, I am amazed how God has used me to His and my advantage. In retrospect, I can understand how the timing and sequence of my life's events were to my ultimate benefit, though I didn't appreciate struggling through at the time. Unfortunately, wisdom and insight can be elusive. Or, do we fail to recognize them through lack of mindfulness?

Without doubt, writing this book allowed me to increase my creative self-awareness and understanding. But don't assume because I write down my feelings and observations on paper it's effortless for me to deal with obstacles occurring in my own life. It is not. No person has all the answers. Everyone battles to cope with the daily conflicts life brings. One constant we can depend on is there will be plenty of challenges during our existence. We may not be able to change the situations we encounter, but we can change our attitude and response to them by staying calm, flexible and open-minded.

It's my hope reading these pages help you in your journey to gain wisdom, understanding and enlightenment into your own creativity and spirit. My wishes for you are these: You will share and inspire others with your voice and art. You will have the courage to experiment freely. You will stay flexible, have fun and discover new creative roads to travel. You will remember to stand back as you look upon life's design wall and clearly see the whole picture. You will deepen your own love of beauty in nature, all things artistic and most importantly, yourself.

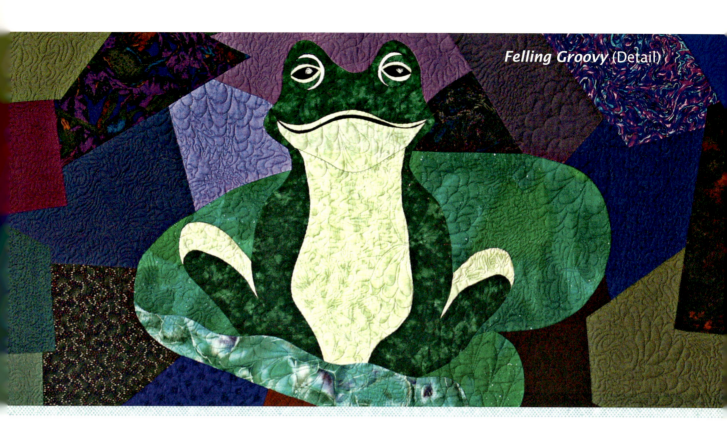

Felling Groovy (Detail)

Happy journeys!

Information and Websites of Interest:

Vikki Pignatelli: www.vikkipignatelli.com

Sacred Threads Quilt Exhibitions: www.sacredthreadsquilts.com

Beyond the Barrier Special Exhibit: http://beyondthebarrier.org

Hand dyed fabrics by Judy Robertson: www.justimagination.com

The Alzheimer's Art Quilt Initiative is a national, grassroots organization whose mission is to raise awareness and fund research through art: www.alzquilts.org

The Alliance for American Quilts-Save Our Stories: www.allianceforamericanquilts.org/qsos. Search for "The Sacred Threads QSOS"

With Sacred Threads: Quilting and the Spiritual Life: (book) by
Susan Towner-Larsen and Barbara Brewer Davis. Pilgrim Press
ISBN: 0-8298-1384-5 or ISBN-13: 9780829813845

Within Sacred Circles: Meditations and Mandala Quilts: (book) by Susan Towner-Larsen
ISBN: 0-8298-1533-3 or ISBN-13: 9780829815337

Merry Yee Clark (graphic design): merryyeedesign@gmail.com

DragonThreads Publishing Company (Worthington, OH): www.dragonthreads.com

The Wonderfil Specialty Thread Company (Calgary, Alberta, Canada): www.wonderfil.net

Quilter's Newsletter Magazine: www.quiltersnewsletter.com

Susan Hart (Sew-n-Save) : www.wsewnsave.com

Inquiries should be addressed to:

Vikki Pignatelli
vikki@vikkipignatelli.com
www.vikkipignatelli.com

Other books and DVDs by Vikki available through her website:

Quilting Curves (Quilt Digest Press, 2001) ISBN: 0-8442424-9-7
Quilting by Improvisation (Dragon Threads, 2006) ISBN: 0-9641201-9-4
Crazy About Curves DVD (2009)

Index of Quilts

After the Storm	47, 48, 50
Aftermath	24
Against All Odds	32, 34
At Sea	120
Blacklick Pond: Reflections At Twilight	29
Breaking Point	17, 18, 49
Child's Play	51
Creation of the Sun and Stars	53, 55, 59
Dreamcatcher	151
Engulfed	106
Feelin' Groovy	27, 149
Fire and Ice	23, 25
Firestorm	138
Hanging on for Dear Life	100, 102
Life Beyond	111, 112
Lightning Strikes Twice	19
Log Cabin Images: A Study In Copper	134
My First Quilt	14
November Moon	96, 97
Passages of the Spirit	8-9, 99, 146
Pond Reflections at Dawn	76, 78
Poppies	140, 141
Portrait of My Soul	41, 42, 43
Red Sky at Night	34
Resting Place	71, 72
Rhapsody in Pink	84, 90
Rocky Mountain Wildflowers	89
Running in Circles	95
Silhouette	39
Summer's Bounty	3, 115
Tears On Blacklick Pond	36, 38
The Fire Within: Our Spirit of Creativity	5, 64, 66
The Promise of Spring	10, 123, 124, 125
The Spider's Web	130, 131
Valley of Fire	128
Windows	143

Some quilts feature multiple openings. They are *Dreamcatcher, Windows, The Spider's Web, Engulfed* and *Summer's Bounty.*

Dreamcatcher (24″ x 27″)

About the Author

Vikki entered the world of quilting in 1991. A non-sewer at the time, Vikki attended a beginner's class at the insistence of her sister, Augustine Ellis, and quickly fell in love with the art of quilting. Now a full-time professional quilt-artist, designer, international teacher, lecturer and author, Vikki and her quilts have been featured in many books, national publications and exhibitions. She has won 32 awards in national and international competitions and exhibitions.

A self-taught artist with experience in painting (watercolor and oils), sculpture and many craft mediums, Vikki enjoys a passion for color and flowing designs. She developed a simple layering technique that is a blend of piecing and appliqué. She is the author of two books featuring this technique, as well as "how-to" articles published in Quilter's Newsletter, AQS and Quilting Arts magazines.

Vikki is also the founder (1998) of the national *Sacred Threads Quilt Exhibitions*, a biennial, two-week display of original artwork exploring emotional and spiritual themes.

Deeply influenced by her husband's bout with cancer and his recovery in 1993, most of Vikki's artwork now focuses on the themes of healing, spirituality, hope, and inspiration. In her writings and teaching, Vikki's intent is to encourage, nurture and develop the artistry and self-confidence within each quilter.

Vikki lives in Reynoldsburg, Ohio, where she resides with Denny, her husband of 44 years. They are blessed with two children, Denise and Dan, and three grandchildren. Vikki and her husband love to travel and dance for relaxation.